I. INTRODUCTION

Over the past year, our nation has continued to take action to combat terrorism both overseas and at home. Together with the Congress, the Administration has passed landmark legislation to reorganize the federal government, aggressively pursued terrorists around the world, improved our intelligence capabilities, enhanced security at our airports, seaports, land borders and local communities, and strengthened America's response capabilities.

Consistent with the requirements of Fiscal Year 1998 National Defense Authorization Act, the fifth annual *Report to Congress on Combating Terrorism* (hereafter referred to as the "Report") details government-wide spending to combat terrorism. As the Report demonstrates, the Federal government has taken decisive action since September 11, 2001 to protect the nation and combat terrorism overseas. In compliance with the Homeland Security Act of 2002, future Reports will be transmitted with the President's Budget.

Federal funding to protect the nation and combat terrorism overseas has dramatically increased since September 11, 2001. In the FY 2004 request, funding for combating terrorism activities increases by 83 percent over FY 2002, the pre-September 11 level. The President's FY 2004 Budget would more than double the pre-September 11 funding level for homeland security, the domestic subset of combating terrorism. And funding for overseas combating terrorism, which includes ongoing efforts to prepare for, protect against, detect, and disrupt terrorism overseas, but does not include direct military action in support of the war on terrorism, would increase by 38 percent over the pre-September 11 level.

Our success in combating terrorism overseas and protecting the homeland is not measured by how much we spend but by how much we accomplish. We will continue to focus our efforts on strategic action and target our resources to mitigate the threats to, and vulnerabilities of, our nation. Over the past year, the Administration has completed a number of strategic documents to guide efforts to combat terrorism, including:

- *The National Strategy for Homeland Security*
- *The National Strategy for Combating Terrorism*
- *The National Strategy to Combat Weapons of Mass Destruction*
- *The National Strategy for the Physical Protection of Critical Infrastructures and Key Assets*
- *The National Strategy to Secure Cyberspace*

To demonstrate how these activities fit into a framework for strategic action, this year's Report has been restructured to mirror the strategic mission areas as delineated in the *National Strategy for Homeland Security*. One of the key challenges that the Report underscores is measuring progress both in terms of outputs and outcomes to benchmark efforts to achieve strategic goals. Much work remains to be done in this area.

The Report is intended to provide Congress insight into how our nation's efforts to combat terrorism are progressing and how the Administration proposes to enhance these efforts. As President Bush said in the *National Strategy for Homeland Security*, "We will not achieve these goals overnight…[but] we will prevail against all who believe they can stand in the way of America's commitment to freedom, liberty, and our way of life."

Reporting Requirement

Section 1051 of the Fiscal Year 1998 National Defense Authorization Act (P.L. 105-85) requires that the Administration provide information on executive branch funding to combat terrorism. Subsequent legislation (section 1403 of P.L. 105-261) requires an annex to this Report on domestic preparedness. Since domestic preparedness is a part of the mission to combat terrorism and is largely captured in the Emergency Preparedness and Response section, we address domestic preparedness aspects of combating terrorism throughout the Report rather than providing a separate annex. The legislation also requires a classified annex providing additional detail on funding.

Scope and Methodology

This Report provides funding and programmatic information on the executive branch's efforts to combat terrorist activity both domestically and overseas. Throughout the FY 2004 budget process, the Office of Management and Budget (OMB) collected three-year funding estimates and associated programmatic information from all federal agencies with responsibility for the combating terrorism mission. These estimates do not include the efforts of the legislative or judicial branches.

Throughout the data collection cycle, agencies reported information using applicable definitions. The data provided by the agencies[1] are developed at the "activity level," which is a set of like programs or projects that make up a coherent effort, aggregated at a level of detail sufficient to analyze total governmental spending on homeland security and overseas combating terrorism missions (the two major components of the overarching combating terrorism mission). OMB purposely left the definition of "activity" to the interpretation of respondent agencies to allow for flexibility in responses, and reviewed all responses to ensure consistency and comparability.

Agencies further categorized their funding data based on the six strategic mission areas defined in the *National Strategy for Homeland Security*, as discussed below. In addition, agencies identified activities from which reported funding supports efforts to defend against terrorist use of weapons of mass destruction (WMD), improve critical infrastructure protection (CIP) efforts, or provide for federal continuity of operations (COOP) in the event of a national emergency. Definitions of these activity-level characterizations are discussed below. For classification purposes, we continue to combine the funding amounts for the Department of Defense and the intelligence community. This funding is labeled throughout the Report as *Defense*.

To the greatest extent possible, this Report maintains programmatic/funding consistency with last year's Report (the year the report was expanded to include all border and aviation security activities as part of the homeland security definition) and the estimates provided in the FY 2004 Budget and Mid-Session Review. Small discrepancies from figures reported in earlier years versus this year's Report are due to agencies' improved ability to extract terrorism-related activities from host programs and refine their characterizations. Furthermore, the Administration

---

[1] In the Report, the term "agency" refers to federal, and federally-affiliated, and federally-assisted entities included as agencies in the President's Budget.

may refine mission area estimates over time based on additional analysis or changes in the way specific activities are characterized and aggregated or disaggregated.

Definitions

Combating terrorism activities include both antiterrorism (defensive measures used to combat terrorism) and counterterrorism (offensive measures used to combat terrorism), both domestically and abroad. Combating terrorism is divided into two primary categories, homeland security (HS) and overseas combating terrorism (OCT), and encompasses all funding for defense against WMD, improvements to CIP, and provision for federal COOP. The following exhibit illustrates the relationship of combating terrorism funding types:

COMBATING TERRORISM

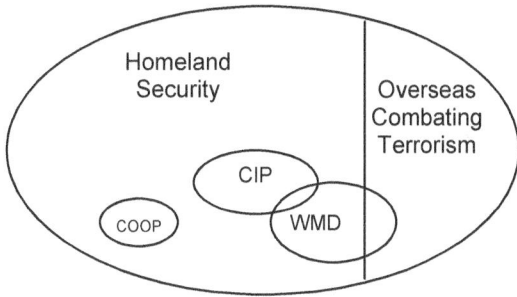

NOTE: Not drawn to funding scale.

Homeland security programs focus on activities within the United States and its territories, or on activities in support of domestically-based systems and processes. The Homeland Security Council (HSC) coordinates these activities government-wide. Overseas combating terrorism focuses on activities outside the United States. The National Security Council (NSC) coordinates these activities government-wide. Together, the two areas comprise the overall combating terrorism budget for the federal government.

Homeland security is defined as a concerted national effort to prevent terrorist attacks within the United States, reduce America's vulnerability to terrorism, and minimize the damage and recover from attacks that do occur. To assist agencies in reporting, OMB has specified that this includes activities that focus on combating and protecting against terrorism that occurs within the United States and its territories (this includes CIP and COOP), or outside the United States and its territories if they support domestically-based systems or activities (e.g., pre-screening high-risk cargo at overseas ports). Such activities include efforts to detect, deter, protect against, and, if needed, respond to terrorist attacks.

For the first time, this report categorizes homeland security activities into the six critical mission areas laid out in the *National Strategy for Homeland Security*. These categories supplant categorizations from past Reports. The mission areas, with definition summaries, are listed below:

- Intelligence and Warning – Terrorism depends on surprise. This mission area includes intelligence programs and warning systems that can detect terrorist activity before it manifests itself in an attack so that proper preemptive, preventive, and protective action can be taken. Specifically, this mission area is made up of efforts to identify, collect, analyze, and distribute source intelligence information or the resultant warnings from intelligence analysis. As part of the homeland security category, this funding excludes intelligence activities of the national security community that are focused overseas.

- Border and Transportation Security – This mission area includes border and transportation security programs designed to fully integrate homeland security measures into existing domestic transportation systems. Since current systems are intertwined with the global transport infrastructure, virtually every community in America is connected to the world by seaports, airports, highways, pipelines, railroads, and waterways that move people and goods in to, within, and out of the nation. This mission area focuses on programs to promote the efficient and reliable flow of people, goods, and services across borders, while preventing terrorists from using transportation conveyances or systems as weapons, or to deliver implements of destruction.

- Domestic Counterterrorism – This mission area incorporates federal funding for any law enforcement programs (including state, local, or regional) that investigate and prosecute criminal activity to prevent and interdict terrorist activity within the United States. It includes all homeland security programs that identify, halt, prevent, and prosecute terrorists in the United States. It also includes pursuit not only of the individuals directly involved in terrorist activity, but also their sources of support: the people and organizations that knowingly fund the terrorists and those that provide them with logistical assistance.

- Protecting Critical Infrastructures and Key Assets – An attack on one or more pieces of our critical infrastructure may disrupt entire systems and cause significant damage. Programs that improve protection of the individual pieces and the interconnecting systems that make up our critical infrastructure belong in this mission area. Any funding for programs associated with the physical or cyber security of federal assets also belongs in this mission area. This mission area also includes programs designed to protect America's key assets, which are those unique facilities, sites, and structures whose disruption or destruction could have significant consequences, including national monuments and icons.

- Defending Against Catastrophic Threats – This mission area includes homeland security programs that involve protecting against, detecting, deterring, or mitigating the terrorist use of weapons of mass destruction, including understanding terrorists' efforts to gain access to the expertise, technology, and materials needed to build chemical, biological, radiological, and nuclear (CBRN) weapons. In addition, this mission area includes funding for efforts or planning to decontaminate buildings, facilities, or geographic areas after a catastrophic event.

- Emergency Preparedness and Response – This mission area includes programs that prepare to minimize the damage and recover from any future terrorist attacks that may occur despite our best efforts at prevention. This area includes programs that help to plan, equip, train, and practice the needed skills of the varied and necessary first responder units, including such groups as police officers, firefighters, emergency medical providers, public works personnel, and emergency management officials. This area also includes programs that will consolidate federal response plans and activities to build a national system for incident management in cooperation with state and local government.

Overseas combating terrorism includes activities that focus on combating and protecting against terrorism that occurs outside the United States and its territories. Such activities include efforts to detect, deter, protect against, and, if needed, respond to terrorist attacks. Overseas combating terrorism does not include funding in support of the war on terrorism or other international conflicts.

Critical infrastructure protection (CIP) enhances the security of those physical and cyber-based systems essential to national security, national economic security, and public health and safety.

Continuity of operations (COOP) are those federal agency activities that ensure the mission essential functions of each agency continue no matter the cause of the disruption, even in the face of a catastrophic event.

Because the *National Strategy for Homeland Security* included protecting critical infrastructure components and key assets in its definition of homeland security – a category that largely encompasses the historical definitions of CIP and COOP – these activities are included in the overall combating terrorism definition (excluding the Department of Defense CIP and COOP funding[2]). However, readers can calculate estimates consistent with previously-reported levels by subtracting CIP and COOP activities from the overall combating terrorism total.

It is important to note that funding levels for all programs in this Report are shown including any fees or collections (that is, this Report shows gross, not net, funding levels). This is because the purpose of this Report is to analyze total government expenditures on the combating terrorism

---

[2] The Department of Defense's (DOD) CIP and COOP efforts are not included in either the homeland security totals or the overseas combating terrorism totals. This is because of the unique nature of DOD's military missions, which are not included within the combating terrorism definition, as well as the difficulty in categorizing DOD CIP and COOP activities as primarily domestically-based or overseas. Furthermore, since DOD's military activities conducted during the reporting period could have dramatically altered CIP and COOP estimates based on constantly-changing conflict conditions, it was impossible to develop accurate estimates. Data reported by DOD in the homeland security/protecting critical infrastructure and key assets mission area may include some of the activities previously reported by DOD as CIP, as well as other activities, but should not be construed as comparable with DOD's historically-reported CIP levels.

mission, not only those funds provided in the annual appropriations process. In addition, funds reported include mandatory funding estimates.

The Data Collection and Dissemination Process

Collecting data on overseas combating terrorism activities and homeland security is difficult because agencies often do not report these activities distinct from other programs. Instead, funding is embedded in larger, "host" programs in agency budget requests. In addition, the Congressional budget process does not typically make explicit appropriations for the combating terrorism mission. Instead, agencies often make specific allocations for these activities after Congress enacts appropriations.

To ensure the availability of information, OMB requested agencies report funding organized by activities that specifically contribute to the combating terrorism mission. To improve transparency, for FY 2004 OMB incorporated combating terrorism estimates into the database that supports the President's Budget. This action has allowed stakeholders to work with aggregated funding data earlier in the process and has given them more flexibility to analyze the funding estimates in both traditional and new ways.

In addition to the information provided in the FY 2004 Budget, OMB has prepared updated summaries of the homeland security and overseas combating terrorism funding estimates for Congress throughout the appropriations cycle. For FY 2005, this Report will be prepared to comply with the requirements of the Homeland Security Act of 2002.

The Establishment of the Department of Homeland Security

The most significant change in this year's Report, both in presentation terms and programmatic analysis, is the inclusion of the new Department of Homeland Security (DHS). On November 25, 2002, the President signed the Homeland Security Act of 2002 (P.L. 107-296), which established DHS and inaugurated the largest reorganization of the federal government since the creation of the Department of Defense in 1947. DHS is a cabinet-level department into which 22 different entities have been consolidated into four major directorates: Information Analysis and Infrastructure Protection, Science and Technology, Border and Transportation Security, and Emergency Preparedness and Response.

As the chart below illustrates, the creation of DHS incorporated half of the government's homeland security funding within a single agency (funding shown is for FY 2003 enacted, the last year for which a pre-/post-DHS comparison is available):

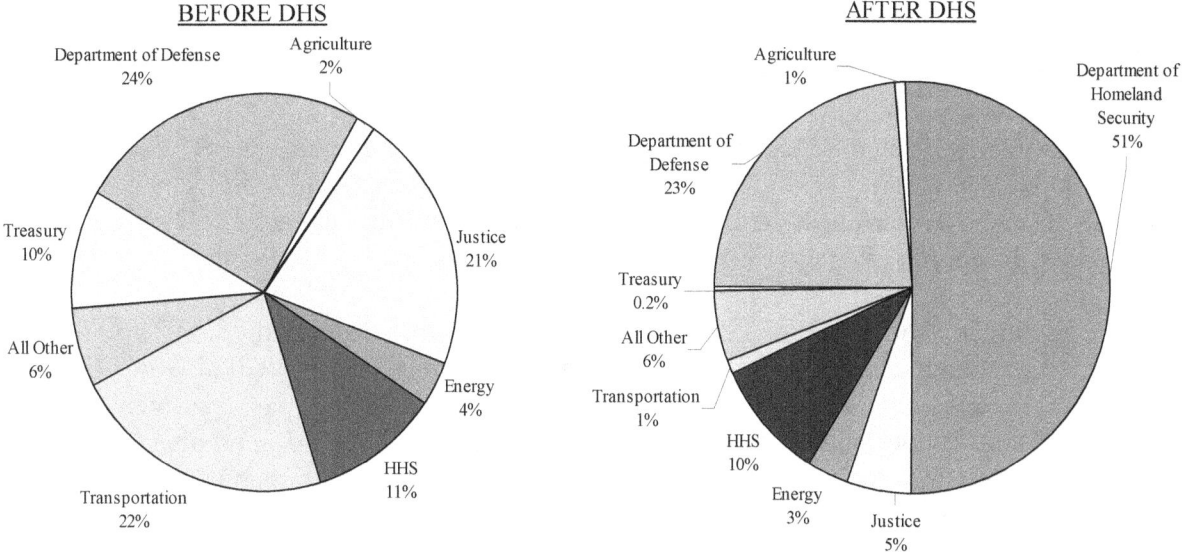

BEFORE DHS

AFTER DHS

In FY 2004, based on the President's request, the percentage of government-wide homeland security funding attributable to the Department of Homeland Security would increase to almost 60 percent.

The following list, organized by DHS directorate, displays programs that were merged into DHS but had previously reported over $100 million in homeland security funding:

Border and Transportation Security
- Justice/Immigration and Naturalization Service
- Justice/Office for Domestic Preparedness
- Treasury/U.S. Customs Service
- Agriculture/Animal and Plant Health Inspection Service (agricultural inspection functions)
- GSA/Federal Protective Service
- Transportation/Transportation Security Administration

Emergency Preparedness and Response
- Federal Emergency Management Agency/formerly an independent agency
- Health and Human Services/Strategic National Stockpile, and the National Disaster Medical System

Science and Technology
- Defense/National Bio-Weapons Analysis Center

Information Analysis and Infrastructure Protection
- Defense/National Communications System

U.S. Coast Guard
- Transportation/U.S. Coast Guard

<u>U.S. Secret Service</u>
- Treasury/U.S. Secret Service

Like the FY 2004 Budget, this Report displays three-year comparable estimates (FY 2002-FY 2004) for homeland security activities transferred to DHS. These activities are displayed in the new DHS structure, which allows readers to compare homeland security activities and funding estimates for the entire period covered by the Report.

DHS was established to empower a single Cabinet official whose primary mission is to protect our homeland, eliminate unnecessary duplication, and ensure that federal activities are conducted in a coordinated and effective way. Later sections of the Report discuss the department's progress and some of its challenges in fulfilling its mission. This year's Report also provides a succinct, tabular description of agencies' and bureaus' major roles and missions. These analyses are intended to provide insight into the framework for federal efforts, and how various agencies contribute to it.

II. FUNDING OVERVIEWS

Below are overviews of the major categories and subcategories of funding, beginning with the broadest category: combating terrorism.

FUNDING OVERVIEW – COMBATING TERRORISM

Total Combating Terrorism Funding by Agency
(budget authority in millions of dollars)

	2002 Enacted	2002 Supplemental	2003 Enacted	2003 Supplemental	2004 Request
Department of Agriculture	230.5	322.2	385.0	110.0	368.2
Department of Commerce	96.8	18.7	110.3	---	153.4
Department of Defense	11,153.0	3,047.0	17,550.0	---	15,172.0
Department of Energy	1,232.9	303.1	1,482.3	77.5	1,588.1
Department of Health and Human Services	434.0	1,479.4	3,602.8	142.0	3,775.5
Department of Homeland Security	11,398.6	5,981.5	19,058.7	4,305.0	23,890.9
Department of Housing and Urban Development	1.0	---	2.0	---	2.0
Department of the Interior	14.6	92.6	110.9	25.0	114.8
Department of Justice	1,018.7	1,124.4	1,973.8	457.2	2,289.4
Department of Labor	71.4	5.9	69.4	---	67.2
Department of State	1,693.1	330.6	1,871.3	214.0	2,365.7
Department of Transportation	634.5	784.4	382.8	---	282.9
Department of the Treasury	85.0	31.7	80.0	---	90.4
Department of Veterans Affairs	47.0	2.0	147.2	---	145.0
Corps of Engineers-Civil Works	---	139.0	36.0	39.0	104.0
Environmental Protection Agency	12.5	175.0	107.7	---	123.1
Executive Office of the President activities	2.0	138.0	43.0	---	37.0
General Services Administration	46.4	51.0	94.6	---	95.7
International Assistance Programs	88.6	483.0	701.3	969.6	1,157.3
National Aeronautics and Space Administration	114.0	109.0	163.0	---	170.0
National Science Foundation	239.9	19.6	284.6	---	307.5
Office of Personnel Management	2.5	---	3.0	---	3.0
Social Security Administration	113.0	8.0	132.0	---	147.0
District of Columbia	13.0	200.0	25.0	---	15.0
Federal Communications Commission	---	---	1.0	---	1.0
National Archives and Records Administration	7.0	3.0	11.0	---	12.0
National Capital Planning Commission	---	1.0	---	---	---
Nuclear Regulatory Commission	6.5	36.4	35.3	---	53.2
Postal Service	---	587.0	---	---	---
Smithsonian Institution	62.5	27.8	82.8	---	80.1
United States Holocaust Memorial Museum	7.0	---	8.0	---	8.0
Corporation for National and Community Service	29.0	---	57.0	---	118.0
Total, Combating Terrorism Budget Authority	**28,854.9**	**15,501.4**	**48,611.6**	**6,339.3**	**52,737.2**

- 32 agencies reported combating terrorism funding in one or more years.

- The FY 2004 request is 83 percent above the FY 2002 enacted[3] level. Fourteen agencies are requesting more than double their FY 2002 enacted level.

- For FY 2004, 18 agencies are requesting an increase over FY 2003. The largest dollar increase is for DHS (+$4.8 billion). Eight agencies are requesting percentage increases of more than 15 percent, totaling $6.3 billion over the FY 2003 enacted level. The largest decline is in DOD (-$2.4 billion, as a result of one-time funding for force protection enhancements in FY 2003).

---

[3] Unless otherwise noted, enacted levels exclude supplemental funding, consistent with tabular presentations.

- Based on the FY 2004 request, DHS (45 percent) and DOD (29 percent) account for close to three-fourths of the total. Another five agencies are requesting more than one percent of the total, and account for a combined 21 percent of the FY 2004 request. The remaining 25 agencies represent less than five percent of the total request.

FUNDING OVERVIEW – HOMELAND SECURITY

Total Homeland Security Funding by Agency
(budget authority in millions of dollars)

	2002 Enacted	2002 Supplemental	2003 Enacted	2003 Supplemental	2004 Request
Department of Agriculture	230.5	322.2	385.0	110.0	368.2
Department of Commerce	96.8	18.7	110.3	---	153.4
Department of Defense	4,426.0	733.0	8,863.0	---	6,717.0
Department of Energy	1,067.2	153.1	1,251.5	77.5	1,362.1
Department of Health and Human Services	434.0	1,479.4	3,602.8	142.0	3,775.5
Department of Homeland Security	11,398.6	5,981.5	19,058.7	4,305.0	23,890.9
Department of Housing and Urban Development	1.0	---	2.0	---	2.0
Department of the Interior	14.6	92.6	110.9	25.0	114.8
Department of Justice	1,018.7	1,124.4	1,973.8	457.2	2,289.4
Department of Labor	71.4	5.9	69.4	---	67.2
Department of State	438.2	38.6	632.7	1.4	811.8
Department of Transportation	634.5	784.4	382.8	---	282.9
Department of the Treasury	85.0	31.7	80.0	---	90.4
Department of Veterans Affairs	47.0	2.0	147.2	---	145.0
Corps of Engineers-Civil Works	---	139.0	36.0	39.0	104.0
Environmental Protection Agency	12.5	175.0	107.7	---	123.1
Executive Office of the President activities	2.0	138.0	41.0	---	35.0
General Services Administration	46.4	51.0	94.6	---	95.7
National Aeronautics and Space Administration	114.0	109.0	163.0	---	170.0
National Science Foundation	239.9	19.6	284.6	---	307.5
Office of Personnel Management	2.5	---	3.0	---	3.0
Social Security Administration	113.0	8.0	132.0	---	147.0
District of Columbia	13.0	200.0	25.0	---	15.0
Federal Communications Commission	---	---	1.0	---	1.0
National Archives and Records Administration	7.0	3.0	11.0	---	12.0
National Capital Planning Commission	---	1.0	---	---	---
Nuclear Regulatory Commission	6.5	36.4	35.3	---	53.2
Postal Service	---	587.0	---	---	---
Smithsonian Institution	62.5	27.8	82.8	---	80.1
United States Holocaust Memorial Museum	7.0	---	8.0	---	8.0
Corporation for National and Community Service	29.0	---	57.0	---	118.0
Total, Homeland Security Budget Authority	**20,618.7**	**12,262.4**	**37,751.9**	**5,157.1**	**41,343.0**

- 31 agencies reported homeland security funding in one or more years.

- The FY 2004 budget request is more than double the FY 2002 enacted level.

- For FY 2004, 12 agencies request more than double their FY 2002 enacted levels. The largest dollar increases are for DHS ($12.5 billion, or 110 percent), Health and Human Services ($3.3 billion, or 770 percent), and Justice ($1.3 billion or 125 percent). An additional five agencies request between a 50 and 100 percent increase over FY 2002.

- Including DOD, the FY 2004 request is 9.5 percent over the FY 2003 enacted level. Excluding DOD, which received one-time funding for force protection enhancements in FY 2003, the FY 2004 request is $5.7 billion (20 percent) over the FY 2003 enacted level.

- In FY 2004, increases of more than $100 million or 15 percent over the FY 2003 enacted level are requested for:

  o DHS (+$4.8 billion, or 25 percent) for enhancements in major mission areas, including: intelligence and warning (+$82 million for intelligence and analytical activities in the Information Analysis and Infrastructure Protection (IAIP) Directorate); border and transportation security (+$508 million, including increases for the US VISIT program, the Container Security Initiative (high-risk cargo screening), maritime safety and security teams, sea marshals, and other activities); protecting critical infrastructures and key assets (+$487 million, including increases for IAIP to inventory, assess, and address vulnerabilities to infrastructures and key assets across sectors); emergency preparedness and response (+$3.4 billion, including increases for terrorism preparedness grant programs and the President's Bioshield initiative, which spur the development of innovative countermeasures that could be added to the Strategic National Stockpile), and the Science and Technology Directorate (+$185 million).

  o Department of Justice (+$316 million, or 16 percent) for increases in intelligence and warning (+$38 million), domestic counterterrorism (+$145 million), and protecting critical infrastructures and key assets (+$134 million), largely to enhance the FBI's ability to analyze, investigate, and respond to terrorist threats, including threats to our physical and cyber infrastructure, training state and local law enforcement, and enhancing the department's communications systems.

  o Department of State (+$179 million, or 28 percent) for increases in border and transportation security, mainly for enhancements to the visa processing system, including efforts to incorporate biometrics.

  o Department of Health and Human Services (+$172 million, or 5 percent) for increases in defending against catastrophic threats (+$98 million, largely for bioterrorism research) and emergency preparedness and response (+$74 million, largely for public health preparedness grant programs).

  o Department of Energy (+$111 million, or 9 percent) for increases in protecting critical infrastructures and key assets to enhance the security of the Department's facilities, materials, and information systems.

  o U.S. Army Corps of Engineers (+$68 million, or 188 percent) in protecting critical infrastructures and key assets to implement prioritized protective measures at facilities where a terrorist incident could cause loss of life or severe economic losses.

  o Corporation for National and Community Service (+$61 million, or 107 percent) in emergency preparedness and response to place volunteer members in public agencies and community organizations that prepare communities to prevent, mitigate, and respond to acts of terrorism and other disasters by supporting and engaging citizens in local public safety, public health or preparedness and relief efforts.

o   Department of Commerce (+$43 million, or 39 percent) for increases in a number of mission areas to enhance the emergency weather radio system for use in the event of terrorism, improve export controls, protect its mission critical systems, and develop standards to improve building security and detect radiological materials and use those materials safely.

o   Nuclear Regulatory Commission (+$18 million, or 51 percent) for increased control of radioactive sources and for protection of nuclear power plants through vulnerability assessments, increased inspection, oversight, and exercises.

• Based on the FY 2004 request, DHS funds close to 60 percent of homeland security resources. DHS, Defense, HHS, Justice, and Energy fund 91 percent of the overall total.

Mission Area Overview

The *National Strategy for Homeland Security* divides homeland security into six functional mission areas: Intelligence and Warning, Border and Transportation Security, Domestic Counterterrorism, Protecting Critical Infrastructures and Key Assets, Defending Against Catastrophic Threats, and Emergency Preparedness and Response. FY 2004 requested funding within these mission areas is shown below.

FY 2004 Requested Homeland Security Funding by Mission Area [4]

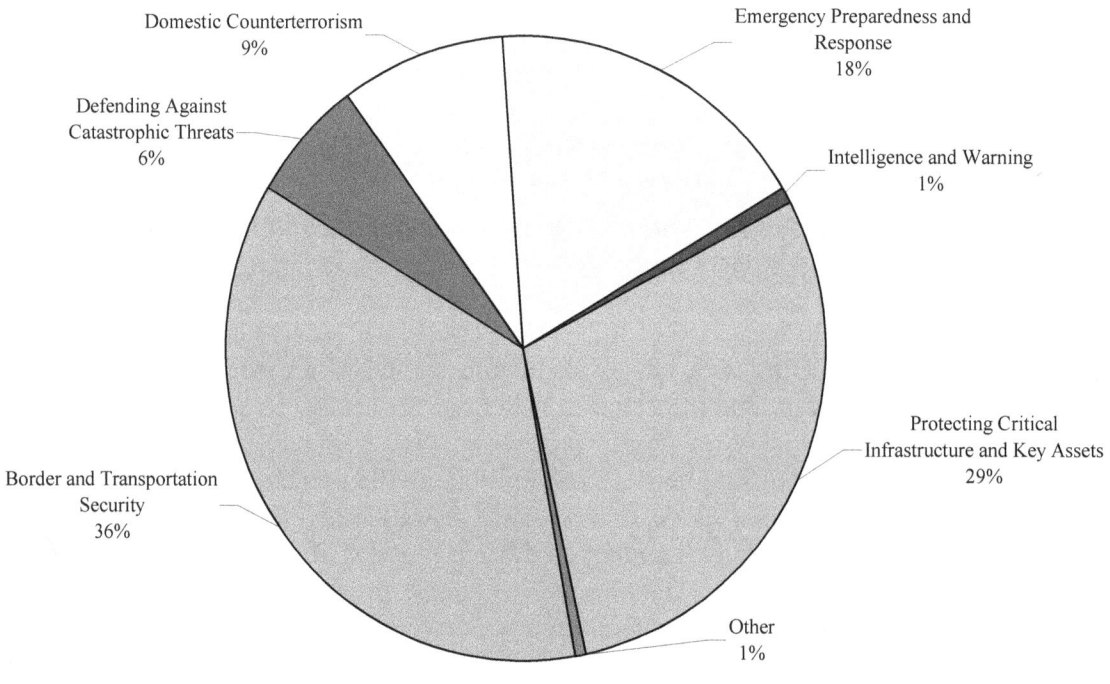

---

[4] "Other" captures those activities that do not fit neatly into the original six mission areas defined in the *National Strategy for Homeland Security*. See separate discussion in the Report.

The largest share ($15 billion total) would fund border and transportation security. Border and transportation security includes most of the activities in DHS' Border and Transportation Security Directorate, including federal activities at ports-of-entry and airports. The mission area with the second largest share ($12 billion total), protecting critical infrastructures and key assets, includes efforts to protect critical infrastructure sectors (e.g., energy, telecommunications) and protection of federal facilities and assets. The third largest share ($7 billion) would be provided for emergency preparedness and response, which includes grant funding for first responder and public health preparedness activities. These mission areas are discussed in greater detail later in the Report.

The table below displays FY 2004 proposed funding by agency and mission area.

FY 2004 Proposed Homeland Security Funding by Mission Area
(budget authority in millions of dollars)

	Border and Transportation Security	Defending Against Catastrophic Threats	Domestic Counter-terrorism	Emergency Preparedness and Response	Intelligence and Warning	Protecting Critical Infrastructure and Key Assets	Other
Department of Agriculture............................	108.8	---	---	15.3	---	244.1	---
Department of Commerce............................	---	72.3	---	29.6	5.5	46.1	---
Department of Defense............................	---	78.0	---	172.0	---	6,467.0	---
Department of Energy............................	---	---	---	89.7	---	1,272.4	---
Department of Health and Human Services.........	---	1,741.5	---	1,851.7	---	182.3	---
Department of Homeland Security..................	14,053.4	674.0	1,973.8	4,875.3	239.6	1,877.4	197.4
Department of Housing and Urban Development..	---	---	---	---	---	2.0	---
Department of the Interior............................	---	---	---	4.2	---	110.6	---
Department of Justice............................	31.1	18.1	1,665.0	2.3	70.0	502.9	---
Department of Labor............................	---	---	---	4.2	---	63.0	---
Department of State............................	779.0	---	---	1.0	---	31.8	---
Department of Transportation........................	67.4	---	21.0	15.2	---	179.3	---
Department of the Treasury............................	---	---	45.2	15.8	2.5	27.0	---
Department of Veterans Affairs......................	---	---	---	16.9	---	128.1	---
Corps of Engineers-Civil Works.....................	---	---	---	---	---	104.0	---
Environmental Protection Agency....................	---	---	---	28.0	---	86.8	8.3
Executive Office of the President activities.........	---	---	---	---	---	---	35.0
General Services Administration.....................	---	---	---	2.0	---	93.6	---
National Aeronautics and Space Administration...	---	---	---	---	---	170.0	---
National Science Foundation.........................	---	27.0	---	---	---	280.5	---
Office of Personnel Management.....................	---	---	---	0.5	---	2.5	---
Social Security Administration.......................	---	---	4.0	---	---	143.0	---
District of Columbia............................	---	---	---	15.0	---	---	---
Federal Communications Commission...............	---	---	---	---	---	1.0	---
National Archives and Records Administration....	---	---	---	---	---	12.0	---
National Capital Planning Commission..............	---	---	---	---	---	---	---
Nuclear Regulatory Commission.....................	---	12.1	---	---	---	41.1	---
Postal Service............................	---	---	---	---	---	---	---
Smithsonian Institution............................	---	---	---	---	---	80.1	---
United States Holocaust Memorial Museum........	---	---	---	---	---	8.0	---
Corporation for National and Community Service.	---	---	---	118.0	---	---	---
Total Homeland Security Budget Authority.....	**15,039.7**	**2,623.0**	**3,709.0**	**7,256.6**	**317.6**	**12,156.5**	**240.7**

Twenty six agencies have reported funding in the protecting critical infrastructures and key assets mission area. This reflects the fact that most entities have reported funding for protection of their own infrastructure. Border and Transportation Security (DHS and State), Domestic Counterterrorism (DHS and Justice), and Intelligence and Warning (DHS and Justice), are largely centralized, with two agencies reporting most of the resources and no more than three other agencies reporting resources. In emergency preparedness and response, DHS and HHS would receive more than 90 percent of the requested resources for their terrorism and public health preparedness activities. However, 16 other agencies report resources in the category, reflecting the fact that many maintain more specialized capabilities to respond to specific threats (e.g., Agriculture if a pest or pathogen was deliberately introduced on a farm).

FUNDING OVERVIEW – OVERSEAS COMBATING TERRORISM

Total Overseas Combating Terrorism Funding by Agency
(budget authority in millions of dollars)

	2002 Enacted	2002 Supplemental	2003 Enacted	2003 Supplemental	2004 Request
Department of Defense	6,727.0	2,314.0	8,687.0	---	8,455.0
Department of Energy	165.7	150.0	230.8	---	226.0
Department of State	1,254.9	292.0	1,238.6	212.6	1,553.9
Executive Office of the President activities	---	---	2.0	---	2.0
International Assistance Programs	88.6	483.0	701.3	969.6	1,157.3
Total, OCT Budget Authority	**8,236.2**	**3,239.0**	**10,859.7**	**1,182.2**	**11,394.2**

- Five agencies reported combating terrorism funding in one or more years.

- The FY 2004 request is 38 percent above the FY 2002 enacted level.

Department of Defense Activities

Three-fourths of the FY 2004 requested OCT funding is in DOD. Reported funding is largely for overseas anti-terrorism/force protection, but includes WMD response, anti- and counter-terrorism training and equipment, and other activities. Estimates do not include direct military activities.

The sensitive, national security nature of the programs that make up the bulk of the OCT resources in DOD and the intelligence community require that the details of those programs be classified. A more in-depth discussion and analysis of these programs can be found in the classified annex of this Report. In general, these programs include:

o *Intelligence Collection, Analysis, and Sharing.* Timely and accurate intelligence is crucial as we unify our efforts to combat terrorism. Through foreign intelligence collection overseas and information sharing with the proper domestic authorities, such as the FBI and DHS, the intelligence community attempts to detect, deter, and disrupt terrorist activity. The intelligence provided by the community can fill information gaps in domestic or overseas threat analysis. Filling the information gaps is crucial to other agencies' ability to detect, deter, and defend against possible future attacks.

o *Offensive Overseas Operations.* The Department of Defense, chiefly through U.S. Special Forces Command, commits a high level of resources to bringing the fight to the terrorist through offensive overseas operations. Offensive operations target terrorist training camps and safe havens, aiming to destroy terrorist foundations and eliminate organizational leaders.

The goal of offensive operations is to destroy the leadership of terrorist organizations, rendering them incapable of mounting effective attacks against the U.S. or others.

o *Personnel Protection.* Protection of the intelligence officers and military personnel conducting overseas combating terrorism missions is vital. Significant resources protect overseas personnel to ensure the success of their missions. DOD provides force protection both to the forces that are permanently assigned and to those forces that are in transit through an area overseas.

Department of State and International Assistance Activities

Fourteen percent of the FY 2004 requested OCT funding is in the Department of State, and an additional ten percent is in International Assistance programs. Funding supports a range of programs to combat terrorism overseas, such as activities that neutralize terrorist financing and training and assistance programs that support other nations' efforts to combat terrorism and increase law enforcement capabilities. In addition, the funds support the protection of U.S. embassies and facilities overseas, as well as efforts to ensure the emergency preparedness of U.S. and foreign governments in the case of a terrorist attack. Requested increases over FY 2003 in FY 2004 include:

- +$125 million in State for overseas facilities security and worldwide upgrades, including physical and cybersecurity enhancements.

- +$33 million in Nonproliferation, Antiterrorism, De-mining and related programs for anti-terrorism assistance, the primary source of antiterrorism training and equipment to the law enforcement organizations of allied nations needing such assistance.

- +$100 million in International Assistance Programs, Foreign Military Financing to train and equip the Afghan National Army and support the U.S. effort to provide internal stability and combat remaining Taliban and *al-Qaida* elements in Afghanistan.

- +$130 million in International Assistance Programs, Foreign Military financing for programs in select additional countries to combat terrorism overseas by enabling allies to bolster border security, combat indigenous terrorist threats, and better support U.S. armed forces.

The war on terrorism has led to a shift in the focus of some programs that have not traditionally had a mission to combat terrorism. As such, targeted Foreign Military Financing, International Military Education and Training, Peacekeeping Operations, International Narcotics and Law Enforcement, and Assistance to the Newly Independent States funding is now classified as overseas combating terrorism, as this funding supports foreign governments' ability to deter, detect, disrupt, and destroy terrorism in their nations and at their borders.

Department of Energy Activities

Energy activities represent two percent of the requested total. Resources support programs to secure nuclear weapons and weapons-usable radiological sources overseas.

Funding to Combat Weapons of Mass Destruction, for Research and Development to Combat Terrorism, to Protect Critical Infrastructure, and to Ensure Continuity of Operations [5]

Combating weapons of mass destruction cuts across the categories above and captures activities to detect, deter, or mitigate the effects of a terrorist attack involving weapons of mass destruction.

Weapons of Mass Destruction Funding by Agency
(budget authority in millions of dollars)

Homeland Security	2002 Enacted	2002 Supplemental	2003 Enacted	2003 Supplemental	2004 Request
Department of Agriculture	134.0	188.8	291.7	110.0	225.5
Department of Commerce	14.7	1.0	14.5	---	19.7
Department of Defense	350.0	25.0	318.0	---	250.0
Department of Energy	722.1	142.6	885.6	71.2	966.4
Department of Health and Human Services	284.8	1,479.4	3,448.6	100.0	3,557.4
Department of Homeland Security	300.4	1,527.3	1,609.0	1,300.0	5,245.0
Department of Justice	15.0	12.9	30.3	6.5	30.4
Department of State	---	12.0	8.0	---	1.0
Department of Transportation	0.7	4.0	---	---	---
National Science Foundation	9.0	---	27.0	---	27.0
Nuclear Regulatory Commission	6.1	35.6	35.1	---	53.1
District of Columbia	---	---	10.0	---	---
Postal Service	---	587.0	---	---	---
Total, Homeland Security WMD	**1,836.7**	**4,015.7**	**6,677.7**	**1,587.7**	**10,375.5**
Overseas Combating Terrorism					
Department of Defense	313.0	---	529.0	---	689.0
Department of Energy	165.7	150.0	230.8	---	226.0
Department of State	1.3	3.6	3.3	---	3.3
Total, Overseas Combating Terrorism WMD	**480.0**	**153.6**	**763.1**	**---**	**918.3**

Research and development (R&D) activities to combat terrorism cut across the categories above and play a role in providing the tools to combat terrorism. The table below displays funding for R&D activities to develop technologies to deter, prevent, or mitigate acts of terrorism.

Research and Development to Combat Terrorism Funding by Agency
(budget authority in millions of dollars)

	2002 Enacted	2002 Supplemental	2003 Enacted	2003 Supplemental	2004 Request
Department of Agriculture	28.0	52.2	30.4	---	42.1
Department of Commerce	11.7	7.0	16.4	---	19.4
Department of Defense	259.0	2.0	597.0	---	157.0
Department of Energy	---	---	19.0	---	---
Department of Health and Human Services	117.2	85.0	831.2	---	1,648.2
Department of Homeland Security	110.0	93.4	658.2	---	844.0
Department of Justice	13.1	76.1	173.5	4.9	174.7
Department of State	1.8	---	1.8	---	1.8
Department of Transportation	54.7	54.0	3.7	---	3.9
Corps of Engineers-Civil Works	---	3.0	---	---	---
Environmental Protection Agency	2.8	1.5	49.7	---	29.0
National Science Foundation	228.8	---	268.5	---	285.7
Postal Service	---	9.5	---	---	---
Total, Combating Terrorism R&D	**827.0**	**383.6**	**2,649.4**	**4.9**	**3,205.7**

---

[5] See CIP and COOP discussion in the introduction.

Critical Infrastructure Protection Funding by Agency
(budget authority in millions of dollars)

	2002 Enacted	2002 Supplemental	2003 Enacted	2003 Supplemental	2004 Request
Department of Agriculture	76.4	185.1	73.2	110.0	91.6
Department of Commerce	19.7	15.9	31.1	---	48.0
Department of Energy	941.2	135.7	1,116.3	77.5	1,257.9
Department of Health and Human Services	147.1	59.3	180.8	---	181.5
Department of Homeland Security	1,813.2	2,467.6	6,016.3	1,825.3	6,256.6
Department of the Interior	11.1	92.6	106.7	25.0	110.6
Department of Justice	121.8	128.9	302.3	32.6	354.5
Department of Labor	65.9	5.9	64.2	---	63.0
Department of State	12.2	1.6	32.9	1.4	31.8
Department of Transportation	448.8	483.0	306.9	---	212.4
Department of the Treasury	17.0	10.0	27.9	---	28.2
Department of Veterans Affairs	27.8	2.0	90.0	---	128.1
Corps of Engineers-Civil Works	---	100.0	36.0	39.0	104.0
Environmental Protection Agency	8.7	135.7	44.9	---	86.8
Executive Office of the President activities	---	56.0	22.0	---	24.0
General Services Administration	45.5	51.0	92.8	---	93.6
National Aeronautics and Space Administration	114.0	109.0	163.0	---	170.0
National Science Foundation	209.7	19.6	222.4	---	251.6
Office of Personnel Management	1.8	---	3.0	---	2.5
Social Security Administration	113.0	8.0	131.8	---	142.8
District of Columbia	---	26.0	---	---	---
National Archives and Records Administration	7.0	3.0	11.0	---	12.0
National Capital Planning Commission	---	1.0	---	---	---
Nuclear Regulatory Commission	6.1	35.6	35.1	---	41.0
Smithsonian Institution	62.5	27.8	82.8	---	80.1
United States Holocaust Memorial Museum	7.0	---	8.0	---	8.0
Total, Homeland Security CIP Budget Authority	**4,277.5**	**4,160.2**	**9,201.2**	**2,110.8**	**9,780.5**

Note: In many cases, CIP funds are used to protect an agency's own assets while some agencies support broader efforts. For example, Smithsonian Institution CIP funds protect internal Smithsonian assets, while significant portions of DHS and Justice funding contributes to external physical and cyber security efforts.

Continuity of Operations Funding by Agency
(budget authority in millions of dollars)

	2002 Enacted	2002 Supplemental	2003 Enacted	2003 Supplemental	2004 Request
Department of Agriculture	1.7	6.5	1.7	---	3.7
Department of Commerce	13.2	1.0	10.2	---	19.6
Department of Health and Human Services	12.7	---	16.2	---	19.4
Department of Homeland Security	26.0	15.0	34.0	15.0	14.0
Department of Housing and Urban Development	1.0	---	2.0	---	2.0
Department of the Interior	3.5	---	4.2	---	4.2
Department of Justice	2.6	8.0	12.9	---	5.7
Department of Labor	5.4	---	5.2	---	4.2
Department of Transportation	5.1	3.7	12.1	---	15.2
Department of the Treasury	21.2	15.0	8.9	---	9.5
Department of Veterans Affairs	17.0	---	26.0	---	7.2
General Services Administration	0.9	---	1.8	---	2.0
Office of Personnel Management	0.8	---	0.0	---	0.5
Social Security Administration	---	---	0.2	---	0.2
Federal Communications Commission	---	---	1.0	---	1.0
Nuclear Regulatory Commission	0.4	0.8	0.2	---	0.1
Total, Homeland Security COOP Budget Authority	**111.5**	**50.0**	**136.6**	**15.0**	**108.6**

III. HOMELAND SECURITY MISSION AREA ANALYSIS

HOMELAND SECURITY:
INTELLIGENCE AND WARNING

Funding Summary – Intelligence and Warning

Intelligence and Warning
(budget authority in millions of dollars)

	2002 Enacted	2002 Supplemental	2003 Enacted	2003 Supplemental	2004 Request
Department of Agriculture............................	---	0.6	---	---	---
Department of Commerce.............................	---	---	---	---	5.5
Department of Homeland Security................	69.4	33.4	112.1	---	239.6
Department of Justice...................................	---	9.2	31.7	104.0	70.0
Department of the Treasury.........................	2.2	---	2.3	---	2.5
Total, Intelligence and Warning............	**71.6**	**43.2**	**146.1**	**104.0**	**317.6**

Major Agency Roles and Missions Summary – Intelligence and Warning

Department/ Agency	Major Agency Roles and Missions
Commerce	*National Oceanic and Atmospheric Administration* • Enhance warning capability of weather radio network
Homeland Security	*Information Analysis and Infrastructure Protection Directorate* • Analyze terrorism-related threat information relevant to homeland security • Associate threat analysis with infrastructures and people • Provide warnings and advisors to agencies, state and local governments, and select critical infrastructure owners and operators *United States Secret Service* • Provide intelligence and advanced analysis for protective operations
Justice	*Federal Bureau of Investigation* • Share intelligence information within the FBI and other federal agencies, as well as state and local authorities *Office of Justice Programs* • Provide counterterrorism training for senior law enforcement

Strategic Context – Intelligence and Warning

To secure the homeland, we should have an intelligence and warning system that can detect terrorist threats and disseminate terrorist-threat information to the proper entities in a timely way; doing so is complex. The identity and location of terrorists may not be known, they may move lawfully and freely through open borders, and indications of their intent may be ambiguous. Furthermore, once we obtain threat information the decision to share information confidentially with a specific infrastructure owner or with the public at large must be made in real-time and in situations with significant uncertainty.

To perform effective intelligence and warning, we should:

- Maintain a tactical threat analysis capability to monitor and analyze terrorist-related intelligence.
- Maintain a strategic threat analysis capability to anticipate and counter terrorist activity.
- Analyze threats and vulnerabilities in a sound manner to facilitate action when appropriate.
- Maintain a reliable system to warn relevant parties and the public of terrorist threats.

The Intelligence and Warning category captures intelligence collection, risk-analysis, and threat-vulnerability integration activities to prevent terrorist attacks. This category also captures warning systems, including the Homeland Security Advisory System (HSAS), which disseminates information regarding the risk of terrorist attacks to federal, state, and local authorities, the private sector, and the American public. Activities in this category often dovetail into domestic counterterrorism and, in some cases, critical infrastructure protection, as agencies move to take immediate action or develop long-term protective measures based on threat or vulnerability information. This category does not include foreign intelligence activities.

Intelligence and Warning Activities

The President's Budget for intelligence and warning activities increases from $72 million enacted in FY 2003 to $318 million proposed for FY 2004. The increase over that period has supported the priorities spelled out in the *National Strategy for Homeland Security*, including: enhancing the analytical capabilities of the FBI, building the capabilities of DHS's Information Analysis and Infrastructure Protection Directorate, and implementing the Homeland Security Advisory System.

Major accomplishments over the past year include establishing two new intelligence units, DHS' Information Analysis and Infrastructure Protection Directorate (IAIP) and the multi-agency Terrorist Threat Information Center (TTIC), as well as additional improvements in the government's ability to monitor and analyze terrorist threats:

- IAIP, DHS' information nerve center, will obtain and analyze intelligence to enhance homeland security. IAIP will also provide the full-range of intelligence support to DHS and manage information collection from other DHS operational components. IAIP's domestic focus will allow it to perform its mission to assess the vulnerabilities of our critical infrastructure and key assets and to map terrorist-threats against those vulnerabilities. IAIP's intelligence activities also support DHS' lead role in issuing warnings, threat advisories, and recommended responses to public safety agencies, elected officials, industry, and the public. IAIP played an important coordinating role during the period of heightened threat in March 2003. IAIP's intelligence and warning activities would grow from $10 million in FY 2002 (prior to the establishment of DHS) to $102 million in FY 2004.

- TTIC, which includes elements from DHS, DOD, State, FBI, and CIA, integrates terrorist threat-related information, collected domestically or abroad, to form a comprehensive threat picture. TTIC will also provide threat analysis and assessments to national leadership and maintain a comprehensive, up-to-date list of known or suspected terrorists. TTIC began operating in May 2003. TTIC is funded from within extant agency homeland security resources.

- FBI will continue to enhance its analytical capability. Funding for FBI's Office of Intelligence, established after September 11 to perform counterterrorism analysis and share intelligence, would grow to $35 million in FY 2004.

Requested increases from FY 2003 (+$172 million, or 117 percent) would build upon the government's efforts to enhance its intelligence and warning capability, and include:

- +$27 million for IAIP's threat determination and assessment program.

- +$54 million for IAIP's information and warning activities. These activities support the Homeland Security Advisory System.

- +$35 million for the Office of Justice Programs to train senior law enforcement in the detection of terrorist groups.

- +$3.3 million for the FBI's Office of Intelligence to ensure intelligence is shared within the FBI and with other federal agencies.

- +$5.5 million for the National Oceanic and Atmospheric Administration (NOAA) to automate the process for collection and dissemination of civil-emergency messages over NOAA Weather Radio.

Challenges

With the addition of the TTIC and IAIP, the Intelligence Community will have to guard against fragmentation of information collection and analysis. The purpose of these entities is to fuse, share, and develop intelligence information and analysis. They will break down information stovepipes that have hindered intelligence efforts in the past. TTIC and IAIP will continue to be sensitive to legal, privacy, and civil liberties concerns.

DHS is responsible for establishing and operating the Homeland Security Advisory System. This system will communicate threat alerts to the general public, government entities, and infrastructure operators. The system must be developed to disseminate alerts in a targeted and timely way, and threat alerts must be further refined to characterize the levels of vigilance and responses such as increasing surveillance of critical locations or closing public facilities.

In building the capabilities of the HSAS and related or other warning systems, DHS will need to remain aware of the potential for overlap and duplication. Many agencies maintain systems to communicate with state and local governments, private sector entities, and citizens. Weather radio, which would be enhanced to support a more comprehensive warning capability, is one such system. In developing homeland security warning capabilities, agencies must coordinate their activities and spending.

HOMELAND SECURITY:
BORDER AND TRANSPORTATION SECURITY

Funding Summary – Border and Transportation Security

Border and Transportation Security
(budget authority in millions of dollars)

	2002 Enacted	2002 Supplemental	2003 Enacted	2003 Supplemental	2004 Request
Department of Agriculture....................................	61.2	31.5	176.6	---	108.8
Department of Homeland Security........................	8,005.0	3,765.0	13,545.0	1,778.0	14,053.4
Department of Justice...	8.1	6.0	25.4	---	31.1
Department of State..	426.0	25.0	591.8	---	779.0
Department of Transportation.............................	537.3	703.0	241.3	---	67.4
Department of the Treasury.................................	8.0	---	---	---	---
Total, Border and Transportation Security.....	**9,045.7**	**4,530.5**	**14,580.1**	**1,778.0**	**15,039.7**

Major Agency Roles and Missions Summary – Border and Transportation Security

Department/ Agency	Agency Roles and Missions
Agriculture	*Animal and Plant Health Inspection Service* • Perform agricultural quarantine activities and risk analysis at ports of entry
Homeland Security	*Bureau of Customs and Border Protection* • Conduct inspections at ports of entry to detect and prevent illegal people and goods, including agricultural products, from entering the U.S. • Establish information systems to control arrival or departure of people and goods into the U.S. and target high-risk people and goods for further inspection and investigation • Detect, track, intercept and apprehend border threats between ports of entry • Work overseas to strengthen U.S. defenses against illegal smuggling and immigration *Bureau of Immigration and Customs Enforcement* • Investigate and enforce laws against the unlawful presence of people and goods into the U.S. *Bureau of Citizenship and Immigration Services* • Administer the visa petition and immigration process to ensure against issuance of immigration benefits to terrorists or persons who violate immigration laws *Transportation Security Administration* • Perform aviation security activities, including passenger and baggage screening, air marshals, and air cargo security • Develop systems to improve passenger screening and detect dangerous materials • Coordinate development of security measures for non-aviation modes, such as land transportation *United States Coast Guard* • Lead port security activities • Disrupt and interdict illegal maritime activities • Patrol ports and waterways • Screen high-interest vessels • Enforce security zones around key vessels and infrastructure • Place armed sea marshals on high-interest vessels • Conduct port security assessments and develop security plans • Review security assessments and plans of vessels and facilities

State	Administration of Foreign Affairs
	• Administer visa program to ensure against travel into the U.S. by terrorists, persons whose presence may be inimical to U.S. national security interests, or persons who violate immigration laws

Strategic Context – Border and Transportation Security

Securing our border and transportation systems presents a substantial task. Ports-of-entry into the United States stretch across 7,500 miles of land border between the United States and Mexico and Canada and 95,000 miles of shoreline and navigable rivers. Each year more than 500 million persons, 130 million motor vehicles, 2.5 million railcars, and 5.7 million cargo containers must be inspected at the border. The conditions and venues where the tasks are performed vary considerably, from air and sea ports-of-entry in metropolitan New York City with dozens of employees to a two-person land entry point in Montana.

In carrying out these tasks, the government should be sensitive to a variety of priorities such as commercial activity, travel and tourism, in addition to security. Cross border trade is significant: some $1.35 trillion in imports were processed in 2001. DHS needs to find the right balance between the appropriate level of screening and security and the free flow of commerce.

The task of securing our nation does not end at the borders. More than 400 airports with scheduled commercial flights are dispersed throughout the country. More than 600 million commercial airline passengers must be screened annually. Of this, 61 million passengers arrive on some 500,000 international flights each year. The rail and commercial motor transport systems also pose security risks.

To ensure America's border and transportation security, we will:

- Ensure accountability in border and transportation security.
- Create "smart borders" equipped with advanced technology to provide greater security while ensuring the expedient flow of goods, services, and people.
- Increase security of international shipping containers.
- Implement the Aviation and Transportation Security Act of 2001 to achieve a secure air travel system.
- Implement the Maritime Transportation Security Act of 2002 to increase security in our nation's ports.

This category includes all homeland security resources related to border and transportation security-related activities. Activities in this category often dovetail into domestic counterterrorism as agencies take law enforcement action to address potential threats to the homeland that may originate along our border or in our transportation systems. The category also relates to critical infrastructure protection, as transportation is a critical infrastructure sector. Homeland security activity at seaports, for example, is at the nexus of Border and Transportation Security and Protecting Critical Infrastructures and Key Assets mission areas.

Border and Transportation Security Activities

The President's Budget increases funding for border and transportation security activities to $15 billion, an increase of $6 billion (66 percent) from the FY 2002 enacted level. Border and transportation security is the largest mission area, covering over one-third of the overall resources requested for homeland security in FY 2004. Approximately half this funding growth is in Transportation Security Administration (TSA) for aviation security activities. In addition, border and transportation security funding in DHS' Bureau of Customs and Border Protection and U.S. Coast Guard significantly contribute to proposed funding growth. The FY 2004 request for the border and transportation security mission area is $460 million above the FY 2003 enacted level.

Major accomplishments in this mission area include:

- Consolidating a number of border and transportation-related agencies within the Department of Homeland Security to ensure accountability in this critical area. Before this consolidation, security operations along the borders were fragmented with many different organizations patrolling and enforcing laws at the borders. The creation of DHS integrated several of these entities into the Border and Transportation Security (BTS) Directorate – the U.S. Customs Service, the Agricultural Quarantine and Inspection (AQI) program, and INS' inspections program, and U.S. Border Patrol – while also incorporating the U.S. Coast Guard as a distinct entity within DHS, BTS and the U.S. Coast Guard together control approximately 90 percent of the resources in the mission area.

  BTS and the U.S. Coast Guard are responsible for managing who and what enters our homeland in order to prevent the entry of terrorists and the instruments of terror while facilitating the legal flow of people, goods, and services on which our economy depends. The agencies also conduct the border security function abroad to the extent allowed by technology and international agreements. Law enforcement personnel take swift action against those who introduce contraband or violate terms of entry and pose threats to the American people. In addition, the U.S. government continues to work with the international community and the private sector to secure the transportation systems that link American communities to the world, moving people and goods across our borders and throughout the country within hours.

- Creating two operating agencies within BTS to manage the work of this mission area. The Bureau of Customs and Border Protection (BCBP) focuses on border security; while the Bureau of Immigration and Customs Enforcement (BICE) focuses on enforcement of immigration and customs laws inside the United States, and reports most of its funding in the domestic counterterrorism category. Both agencies report to the Under Secretary for BTS.

  BCBP consists primarily of Border Patrol officers and inspectors from the former INS, U.S. Customs Service and AQI. This roughly 42,000-person bureau focuses exclusively on security at and between the ports-of-entry. They provide "one-stop shopping" for people, cargo, and conveyance entering the United States by unifying inspection functions and the chain of command. In the past, people, cargo, and conveyances entering the United States would have been inspected by personnel from multiple agencies. Under this new agency, people, cargo, and conveyances entering the United States experience a seamless inspection process.

- Implementing the Aviation and Transportation Security Act of 2001 by creating the Transportation Security Administration (TSA) which is another critical part of the BTS Directorate. TSA is in control of all passenger screening operations at airports and screens all airline baggage. Over the course of the past year, TSA has successfully hired, trained and deployed a screener workforce to each of the 429 airports with scheduled commercial flights. More than 6,800 baggage screening devices have been deployed to detect weapons and explosives, putting into use the latest technology to protect passengers. All passenger baggage is now screened through such devices or by alternative screening methods. TSA is also using intelligence information and technology more effectively to identify higher-risk passengers. As a result, overlapping layers of screening have been reduced, such as screening at terminal gates. In 2004, the budget includes over $4.8 billion to continue these efforts in the nation's airports.

  In addition to improved passenger and baggage screening, TSA has deployed thousands of federal air marshals on domestic and international flights. TSA has also hardened or replaced approximately 6,000 cockpit doors on commercial aircraft and has begun a program to train and arm pilots.

- Enhancing maritime and port security in key areas. Since September 11, the U.S. Coast Guard has made the largest commitment to port security operations since World War II, including over 35,000 port security patrols and 3,500 air patrols. The U.S. Coast Guard has boarded over 2,500 high-interest vessels and interdicted over 6,200 illegal migrants, and created and maintained over 115 Maritime Security Zones. Coast Guard has also issued regulations designed to protect America's ports and waterways from a terrorist attack by requiring ports, vessels, and facilities to develop security plans and implement needed security measures. DHS is completing threat and vulnerability assessments of United States ports and is deploying teams overseas to ensure that foreign ports have effective security programs.

- Establishing the Container Security Initiative (CSI) with tough new procedures targeting high-risk cargo containers before they embark en route to United States ports. As of August 2003, 18 countries, including Canada, have signed a declaration of principle to participate in the CSI program. Located within the countries who have signed a declaration of principle are 38 ports, of which 16 are operational. The top CSI ports represent approximately two-thirds of the cargo containers coming to the United States. Of these ports, 12 are operational.

- Enrolling thousands of commercial importers in the Customs-Trade Partnership Against Terrorism program (C-TPAT) to secure the entire supply chain. Under C-TPAT, private industry partners providing verifiable security information receive preferential treatment during the shipping process. This allows DHS to devote more of our resources to suspect activities.

24

- Implementing new visa policies improves security. For example, the Department of State developed a new tamper-resistant visa, expanded the visa application review process, enhanced the visa lookout system, and established direct data-sharing connections regarding travelers wishing to visit the United States, thereby improving information sharing among U.S. law enforcement agencies and the intelligence community.

Increases requested for FY 2004 include:

- +$100 million in BCBP funding for the continued development of US VISIT, a comprehensive entry-exit system. This system will establish departure control and improve the arrival inspection process by documenting the entry and exit of visitors to the United States.

- +$167 million in the Department of State funding for border security enhancements, largely to the visa processing system, including efforts to incorporate biometrics (note that this is a fee-funded activity).

- +$62 million in BCBP for the Container Security Initiative, supporting DHS personnel in key international ports to examine high-risk cargo before it is placed on ships bound for the US.

- + $65 million in the U.S. Coast Guard for six new Maritime Safety and Security Teams.

- + $53 million in the U.S. Coast Guard for nine new Coastal Patrol Boats, used for vessel escorts and enhanced presence in port areas.

- + $16 million in BCBP for the Customs Trade Partnership Against Terrorism (C-TPAT), which supports partnerships with importers to improve security along the entire supply chain.

- + $3 million in the U.S. Coast Guard for additional sea marshals. Sea marshals are U.S. Coast Guard personnel placed on commercial ships entering ports to prevent them from being hijacked.

Challenges

Until now, the focus of homeland security initiatives has been on securing our physical boundaries. Tomorrow's focus must be on creating "smart borders" to provide protection by identifying threats before they get near our borders while continuing to facilitate trade. The major challenges are in information technology and fully integrating the components of DHS to create seamless border protection.

For example, a number of major information technology initiatives are underway in the Border and Transportation Security Directorate. The 2004 President's Budget continues support for the Advance Passenger Information System (APIS) that is used by border agencies to transmit identifying data on passengers bound for and departing from the United States. This information is checked against multiple criminal databases, including the National Crime Information Center database maintained by the FBI. In order to overcome the limits of the existing system and to provide more effective and efficient support for aviation security, over $60 million has been devoted to APIS since the attacks of September 11, 2001.

DHS is also continuing to develop and implement the US VISIT system. This project entails significant investment in infrastructure and technology to build a comprehensive and integrated system that will enable it to track both the entry and exit of visitors to the United States. From 2002 through 2004, $860 million will be used to support this initiative. A pilot for US VISIT has already been implemented. It requires visitors who may present an elevated national security concern to provide important information about their visit upon arrival and to confirm their departure from the United States. In addition, expanded electronic information is now required for airline passengers, which enables more accurate entry and exit data to be analyzed on visitors to our country. These major systems projects will be undertaken with a broad understanding of DHS' information architecture requirements, recognizing how the systems should work together to fulfill homeland security requirements and eliminate redundancies.

Other significant challenges remain. Some are logistics and infrastructure related. For example, hiring additional personnel, and making infrastructure improvements at the border to accommodate enhanced security require sufficient time and planning. Other challenges, however, relate to how to best rationalize and consolidate disparate border security organizations into a coherent and focused entity with common missions, goals, and a culture of performance. DHS should implement a unified plan for border "defense in depth" to ensure that border and transportation security organizations communicate, have a common picture of the threat environment, with each other and work together to mitigate risks to our nation in a coordinated way.

Finally, performance measures and goals must be developed to accurately assess efforts in this area and determine the effectiveness of programs to enhance border and transportation security. DHS is currently developing a five year homeland security plan that links program requests with operational measures. In addition, DHS is creating a program and activity structure that is linked to goals, not functions. These efforts will be significant in successfully integrating the budget with critical performance goals and key measures.

HOMELAND SECURITY:
DOMESTIC COUNTERTERRORISM

Funding Summary – Homeland Security/Domestic Counterterrorism

Domestic Counterterrorism
(budget authority in millions of dollars)

	2002 Enacted	2002 Supplemental	2003 Enacted	2003 Supplemental	2004 Request
Department of Homeland Security..............	1,858.2	136.2	1,919.6	156.7	1,973.8
Department of Justice.................................	799.0	708.4	1,519.6	314.1	1,665.0
Department of Transportation.....................	3.0	16.0	1.0	---	21.0
Department of the Treasury........................	30.3	6.7	40.6	---	45.2
Social Security Administration..................	---	---	---	---	4.0
Total, Domestic Counterterrorism........	**2,690.5**	**867.3**	**3,480.8**	**470.8**	**3,709.0**

Major Agency Roles and Missions Summary – Domestic Counterterrorism

Department/ Agency	Agency Roles and Missions
Homeland Security	*Bureau of Immigration and Customs Enforcement* • Enforce laws related to the illegal presence of people and goods within the U.S. • Detain those suspected of immigration-related violations • Remove those convicted of immigration-related violations • Pursue criminal aliens, cases of identity theft or benefit fraud, human trafficking, money laundering, and other violations of such laws • Support federal law enforcement campaign against terrorist financing • Participate in Joint Terrorism Task Forces
Justice	*Federal Bureau of Investigation* • Detect and prevent terrorist acts through analysis and fieldwork to identify terrorists, their supporters, and materials that may be used to perpetrate a terrorist act • Track foreign terrorists and keep them from entering the U.S. • Lead Joint Terrorism Task Forces to increase cooperation between federal, state, and local law enforcement • Lead federal law enforcement campaign against terrorist financing • Maintain capability to investigate terrorist incidents, including those involving WMD *Other Justice bureaus and programs, including:* • Prosecute those accused of terrorist acts • Deny criminals and terrorists access to firearms and explosives • Training agents and prosecutors in terrorist financing investigations and forfeitures
Treasury	*Multiple Bureaus* • Participate in Joint Terrorism Task forces and other related activities • Support federal law enforcement campaign against terrorist financing • Prohibit financial transactions involving terrorists and their sponsors

Strategic Context – Domestic Counterterrorism

The attacks of September 11 and the catastrophic loss of life and property that resulted have redefined the mission of federal, state, and local law enforcement authorities. Preventing and interdicting terrorist activity within the United States has become a priority for federal, state, and local law enforcement. This category includes federal and federally-supported efforts to identify, halt, and, where appropriate, prosecute terrorists in the United States. As is stated above, activities in the intelligence and warning and domestic counterterrorism categories are closely related. The former captures activities that develop the basis for law enforcement action; the later captures activities that are carried out on that basis.

Domestic Counterterrorism Activities

Funding for domestic counterterrorism has increased by over $1 billion (38 percent) from FY 2002 to the FY 2004 request. This increase reflects both the costs of investigating the terrorist attacks of September 11, 2001, as well as funding to increase capabilities to prevent terrorist attacks. Department of Justice funding has more than doubled (+$866 million, or 108 percent) over that period. The FY 2004 Budget requests an increase of $228 million (8 percent) over the FY 2003 enacted level for domestic counterterrorism activities.

Two agencies report 98 percent of the government's Domestic Counterterrorism resources – the Departments of Homeland Security and Justice. These agencies, in collaboration with others, have worked to carry out the priorities from the *National Strategy for Homeland Security*, including improving intergovernmental law enforcement, facilitating the apprehension of potential terrorists, continuing ongoing investigations and prosecutions, restructuring the FBI to emphasize prevention, targeting terrorist financing, and tracking foreign terrorists and bringing them to justice.

In the reorganization creating the Department of Homeland Security, border-related functions were transferred to the Bureau of Customs and Border Protection (BCBP). Other functions of the predecessor agencies, including enforcement activities from the U.S. Customs Service and the Immigration and Naturalization Service, were transferred into the Bureau of Immigration and Customs Enforcement (BICE). BICE now reports the highest level domestic counterterrorism resources of any bureau in the federal government, requesting $1.9 billion (including mandatory funds) in the category for FY 2004.

Within the domestic counterterrorism mission area, BICE focuses on the enforcement of immigration and customs laws within the United States. BICE was created to unify previously-fragmented investigative functions, creating a more cohesive and comprehensive effort to investigate activities that may threaten the nation.

BICE activities in this category include pursuing criminal aliens, identity theft or benefit fraud, smuggling, human trafficking, and money laundering. BICE also ensures the departure from the United States of removable aliens through the enforcement of the nation's immigration laws. Since its inception, BICE has:

- Seized tens of thousands of fraudulent government identity documents with a street value of more than three million dollars.

- Seized art and a cache of weapons that were looted from Iraq and were being transported into the United States.

- In partnership with the Defense Criminal Investigative Service, executed search warrants on 18 U.S. companies as part of an ongoing probe into the illegal export of U.S. military components to a front company in London that procures arms for the Iranian military.

- Participated in a number of investigations involving the illegal sale or export of weapons or military equipment components.

The Department of Justice's most important role in combating terrorism is the prevention of terrorist acts. Through the collection and effective use of intelligence, the department, primarily through the Federal Bureau of Investigation (FBI), detects and prevents terrorist acts before they occur. The FBI, through its investigative programs and the Foreign Terrorist Tracking Task Force, works to uncover "sleeper cells" and their supporters within the United States and to disrupt terrorist financial, communications, and operational lifelines.

Cooperation among law enforcement agencies at all levels represents an important component of a comprehensive response to terrorism. This cooperation assumes its most tangible operational form in the Joint Terrorism Task Forces (JTTFs) that are established in 66 cities across the nation. These task forces are well-suited to prevent and investigate terrorism because they combine the national and international investigative resources of the FBI and other federal agencies with the street-level expertise of local law enforcement agencies. This cop-to-cop cooperation has proven successful in preventing several potential terrorist attacks.

This process of developing information and sharing that information through an effective network has led to a variety of significant accomplishments in domestic counterterrorism over the past year, including:

- Disrupting terrorist cells in Buffalo, Seattle, Portland, Oregon, and North Carolina.

- Referring more than 200 leads to FBI counterterrorism components for further investigation based on analysis of identify information for known or suspected terrorists from the FBI's Foreign Terrorist Tracking Task Force.

The FBI also is the lead agency for investigating terrorist acts that do occur. The FBI investigates terrorist incidents to develop evidence to support the arrest and prosecution of the individuals involved.

Over the past year, the Department of Justice has undergone a number of structural changes that affect its domestic counterterrorism efforts. The Homeland Security Act transferred the Bureau of Alcohol, Tobacco, Firearms, and Explosives (ATF) from the Department of Treasury to the Department of Justice. The ATF transfer will give the Department of Justice more expertise to investigate incidents involving explosives and firearms. Along with other transfers in the Homeland Security Act, this shift consolidated government-wide domestic counterterrorism resources in Justice and DHS.

In addition, Justice has revised its strategic plan and taken other actions to reinforce its counterterrorism program. FBI, for example, has transformed itself to respond to the threat of terrorism. Instead of just investigating past crimes, the agency's 25,000 employees are now focused on preventing future attacks. Since September the 11th, the share of FBI resources dedicated to fighting terror has more than doubled. Renewed emphasis has been placed on modernizing FBI technology to facilitate the collection, analysis, and sharing of information. Finally, the FBI has been restructuring its organization and changing business practices to provide improved management and oversight of its counterterrorism programs.

Requested increases for domestic counterterrorism from FY 2003 include:

- +$87 million for BICE enforcement activities.

- +$18 million for FBI field office technology support.

- +$97 million for FBI counterterrorism field investigations.

- +$6 million for FBI's Critical Incident Response Group, which facilitates coordination in response to major law enforcement crises and special investigations.

- +$3 million for the FBI's hazardous devices school, which provides assistance to federal, state, and local law enforcement.

- +$12 million for the Department of Justice's U.S. Attorneys offices and litigating divisions to prosecute terrorists, pursue homeland-security related cases or investigative matters, and provide expert legal advice and guidance.

Challenges

Despite the progress that has been made, terrorism will continue to be a threat to American citizens for the foreseeable future. In particular, finding terrorists and their supporters already in the United States is a serious intelligence and law enforcement challenge. The Department of Justice, including the FBI, must continue its ongoing efforts to improve their infrastructure and management capacity to meet this challenge. The department must persist in transforming its organization to anticipate terrorist actions based on specific information, as well as assessments of threat and risk, and attempt to measure its performance based on these assessments. It must continue to improve its ability to analyze and share information, both among federal agencies and with state and local law enforcement. BICE must continue to integrate its operations to create a coherent, focused investigative arm for DHS and the federal government. And all federal agencies must work with Congress to fill the legal gaps that could frustrate the efforts of the United States to detect and prevent terrorism.

HOMELAND SECURITY:
PROTECTING CRITICAL INFRASTRUCTURE AND KEY ASSETS

Funding Summary – Protecting Critical Infrastructure and Key Assets

Protecting Critical Infrastructure and Key Assets
(budget authority in millions of dollars)

	2002 Enacted	2002 Supplemental	2003 Enacted	2003 Supplemental	2004 Request
Department of Agriculture	163.6	248.7	196.7	110.0	244.1
Department of Commerce	23.6	16.9	31.3	---	46.1
Department of Defense	4,076.0	708.0	8,545.0	---	6,467.0
Department of Energy	953.3	135.7	1,130.6	77.5	1,272.4
Department of Health and Human Services	147.7	59.3	181.6	---	182.3
Department of Homeland Security	977.7	186.0	1,384.7	240.3	1,877.4
Department of Housing and Urban Development	1.0	---	2.0	---	2.0
Department of the Interior	11.1	92.6	106.7	25.0	110.6
Department of Justice	208.2	128.9	368.7	32.6	502.9
Department of Labor	65.9	5.9	64.2	---	63.0
Department of State	12.2	1.6	32.9	1.4	31.8
Department of Transportation	88.2	48.0	128.0	---	179.3
Department of the Treasury	23.1	10.0	21.9	---	27.0
Department of Veterans Affairs	27.8	2.0	90.0	---	128.1
Corps of Engineers-Civil Works	---	100.0	36.0	39.0	104.0
Environmental Protection Agency	8.7	135.7	44.9	---	86.8
General Services Administration	45.5	51.0	92.8	---	93.6
National Aeronautics and Space Administration	114.0	109.0	163.0	---	170.0
National Science Foundation	231.0	19.6	257.6	---	280.5
Office of Personnel Management	1.8	---	3.0	---	2.5
Social Security Administration	113.0	8.0	132.0	---	143.0
United States Holocaust Memorial Museum	7.0	---	8.0	---	8.0
District of Columbia	---	26.0	---	---	---
Federal Communications Commission	---	---	1.0	---	1.0
National Archives and Records Administration	7.0	3.0	11.0	---	12.0
National Capital Planning Commission	---	1.0	---	---	---
Nuclear Regulatory Commission	6.5	36.4	35.3	---	41.1
Postal Service	---	406.5	---	---	---
Smithsonian Institution	62.5	27.8	82.8	---	80.1
Total, Protecting Critical Infrastructure and Key Assets	**7,376.5**	**2,567.5**	**13,151.6**	**525.8**	**12,156.5**

Major Agency Roles and Missions Summary – Protecting Critical Infrastructure and Key Assets

Department/ Agency	Agency Roles and Missions
Agriculture	Agriculture and Meat and Poultry sector.
Defense	Defense Industrial Base sector.
Energy	Energy sector.
Health and Human Services	All other food products and Public Health sectors.
Homeland Security	Emergency Services, Government, Information and Telecommunications, Transportation, and Postal and Shipping sectors.
Interior	National Monuments and Icons sector.
Treasury	Banking and Finance sector.
EPA	Water sector.

Protecting the nation's critical infrastructures and assets is a complex challenge. Our open society offers an array of potential targets to terrorist attack; these are detailed in the *National Strategy for the Physical Protection of Critical Infrastructures and Key Assets* and the *National Strategy to Secure Cyberspace*. In addition, because more than 85 percent of the nation's critical infrastructure and assets are not federally-owned, effective protection requires cooperation from all levels of government and with private industry. This category captures the efforts of various federal agencies to secure our critical infrastructures from terrorist attacks.

As a result of the Homeland Security Act of 2002, the nation's primary infrastructure protection efforts have been unified within the Department of Homeland Security (DHS). To fulfill its mission, DHS will use a risk-based approach to prioritize its protection programs and activities. DHS will also integrate and coordinate federal infrastructure protection responsibilities. Along with DHS, other federal agencies will continue work together to reduce infrastructure vulnerability to terrorism.

The National Strategy for Homeland Security provides a sector-based scheme for protecting critical infrastructure and key assets. Critical infrastructures and assets are contained within 13 different critical infrastructure sectors. Each sector has unique protection challenges and a lead federal department responsible for that sector. The 13 sectors fall under three broad functions: Essential Goods & Services, Interconnectedness & Operability, and Public Safety & Security.

Critical infrastructure and key resources cannot all be protected at the same level. As such, federal resources and efforts must be focused on protecting the highest priority infrastructures. Securing infrastructure and assets in all sectors will prevent terrorists from:
- Exploiting infrastructure to produce a WMD-like effect;
- Causing long-term economic harm; and
- Damaging the nation's morale.

Agency Highlights for Essential Goods and Services - Protecting Critical Infrastructure and Key Assets

As various federal infrastructure protection efforts were unified within DHS, the department assumed the roles and activities of five separate infrastructure protection offices. The Homeland Security Act combined the Critical Infrastructure Assurance Office, National Infrastructure Protection Center, Federal Computer Incident Response Center, the Office of Energy Assurance, and the National Communications System. In addition, beginning in 2004, DHS will conduct and compile vulnerability assessments of the nation's key infrastructure components and assets; enable effective partnerships with state and local government and with the private sector, and develop a national infrastructure protection plan. DHS' Information Analysis and Infrastructure Protection (IAIP) Directorate will assume the responsibility of implementing, integrating, and coordinating federal infrastructure protection responsibilities.

Despite the creation of DHS, infrastructure protection must also involve close collaboration with other federal agencies such as the Departments of Transportation (DOT), Energy (DOE),

Agriculture, and the Environmental Protection Agency (EPA). These departments have highly specialized expertise and long-standing relationships with industry.

Given the diversity of the transportation sector, DOT has responded to the heightened awareness of possible terrorist attacks for all transportation systems. Physical security assessments were conducted for U.S. waterway infrastructure, resulting in the hardening of lock control houses. The Federal Transit Administration has and will continue to work with local transit agencies to test and deploy integrated intrusion detection technologies in tunnels and open track areas in cities with heavily used transit systems.

Any prolonged interruption of the energy supply – be it electricity, natural gas, or oil products – would be devastating to the nation. DOE is responsible for the coordination of protection activities within the energy sector, including developing and maintaining collaborative relationships with state and local governments and industry. In addition, DOE retains responsibility for the energy emergency support function of the Federal Response Plan. Under this plan, DOE gathers, assesses, and coordinates information on energy system damage resulting from a major emergency or significant event. DOE advises federal, state, and local authorities on energy restoration, assistance, and supply, and assists state and local governments on emergency response activities.

The nation's agricultural resources, a source of essential commodities, are protected by several Department of Agriculture programs. In-house agricultural research, through the Agricultural Research Service (ARS), protects plant and animal resources. ARS programs include the rapid detection of diseases, as well as ongoing research on specific diseases such as African swine fever, avian influenza, hog cholera, and exotic Newcastle disease. Additional funding for USDA research facilities is focused on enhancing their research and animal diagnostic capability.

Increases requested over the FY 2003 enacted level for FY 2004 include:

- +$135 million for DHS to identify and catalog critical infrastructure and key assets and conduct vulnerability and risk assessments of them.

- +$7 million for the Department of Agriculture to improve testing, training, and preparation for biological pathogens.

Agency Highlights for Interconnectedness and Operability - Protecting Critical Infrastructure and Key Assets

Cyberspace is a key element of infrastructure protection because it links many sectors. The consequences of a cyber attack could cascade across the economy, imperiling public safety and national security.

In June 2003, DHS established the National Cyber Security Division to improve security across the federal government and work with industry to secure the nation's major networks. This division will identify risks and help reduce the vulnerabilities to government's cyber assets and coordinate with the private sector to identify and help protect America's critical cyber assets;

oversee a consolidated Cyber Security Tracking, Analysis, & Response Center (C-STARC), which will detect and respond to Internet events; track potential threats and vulnerabilities to cyberspace; coordinate cyber security and incident response with federal, state, local, private sector and international partners; and create, in coordination with other appropriate agencies, cyber security awareness and education programs and partnerships with consumers, businesses, governments, academia, and international communities. In addition, the United States Secret Service efforts in this area include the investigation of fraud, cyber-crime, identity theft, and computer intrusion, thus preventing disruptions to our nation's telecommunications and payment systems. The Secret Service has also spearheaded the creation of 13 Electronic Crimes Task Forces, which are multi-agency teams that combat a series of high-tech crimes that include cyber crime, identity theft, and computer intrusion.

Outside DHS, other federal agencies are working to secure cyberspace through their traditional roles. For example, the Department of Commerce's National Institute of Standards and Technology (NIST) develops standards and guidelines in support of our federal responsibilities for IT security. Over the past several years, NIST has developed the "Common Criteria," which specifies security requirements as well as Role-Based Access Control, a new approach to controlling user access. In addition to its cyber-security work, NIST will continue to field its computer security expert assist team.

The FBI's cyber program prevents, where possible, the exploitation of the Internet, computer systems, or networks as the principal instruments or targets of terrorist organizations or foreign government sponsored intelligence operations. Where such violations of federal law do occur, the FBI uses cyber squads resident in most of the bureau's major field offices. The FBI forms and maintains public and private alliances to maximize its cyber response capabilities. In addition, the FBI is improving its capabilities for cyber investigations overseas, and will send FBI personnel to help investigate cyber crimes when invited or allowed by a host country. The Department of State is assisting in these outreach efforts to make foreign countries increasingly aware of this threat and of the need to cooperate in combating it.

In addition to the activities covered above, approximately $1 billion is devoted to improving the security of the federal government's IT networks. Most, if not all agencies have improved the security of important IT systems that are found in emergency operations centers vital to public health, that deliver services such as pension payments, and that support basic administrative activities.

Increases requested over the FY 2003 enacted level for FY 2004 include:

- +$55 million for DHS to establish the National Cyber Division and operate the Cyber Warning Information Network and the Global Early Warning Information System; and

- +$44 million for FBI to strengthen infrastructure investigative resources in the field.

Agency Highlights for Public Safety and National Security - Protecting Critical Infrastructure and Key Assets

A major component of ensuring public safety and national security is protecting federally-owned, leased, or occupied buildings and federal employees from terrorist attack. In FY 2004, the federal government (excluding DOD) will devote over $2.7 billion for protecting employees, facilities, and property.

Within the Department of Homeland Security a number of entities focus on the physical protection of government assets and key infrastructure. The Federal Protective Service, within the Bureau of Immigration and Customs Enforcement, protects federally-owned or leased properties throughout the country. The U.S. Secret Service's traditional protective responsibilities have expanded to include coordination of site security plans at designated special security events, such as major sporting events, political conventions, and the Olympic Games.

DOD's activities also cover a large portion of federal funding in this area. DOD programs are focused on physical security and improving the military's ability to detect terrorist attacks against soldiers and bases. To support this effort, DOD fields its Joint Chiefs of Staff Integrated Vulnerability Assessment Teams to military installations. Teams are funded to conduct 100 assessments in FY 2004.

DOE's Security Program develops policies and provides programmatic direction governing the protection of DOE assets, including significant quantities of nuclear materials. DOE implements these safeguards and security requirements at its research labs, weapons production facilities, and cleanup sites to prevent terrorist threats from nuclear and radiological weapons.

Along with national security, federal funds are spent on the physical protection of assets to ensure public safety in areas such as aviation (air traffic control facilities), chemical manufacturing (plants), nuclear power (plants), hydropower (dams), and federal assets (federal buildings and federally-owned cyber infrastructure). For example, in FY 2004, DOT's Federal Aviation Administration (FAA) plans to upgrade security at its air traffic control facilities. An attack on the air traffic control system would be disruptive as the FAA monitors 89,000 daily flights.

The U.S. chemical industry has worked with the EPA and DHS to enhance measures in place to ensure the safety of its facilities and to prevent accidental releases. Companies representing more than 90 percent of chemical production have adopted a comprehensive security code that includes mandatory inspections.

As required by the Public Health Security and Bioterrorism and Response Act of 2002, all community water systems serving a population greater than 3,300 must complete vulnerability assessments and emergency response plans. EPA must certify these documents, and to assist in this effort, EPA provides grants and training to municipalities. By September 30, 2003, all community water systems serving a population of 100,000 or greater (45 percent of total community water system customers) are expected to have vulnerability assessments and emergency response plans certified by EPA.

The Nuclear Regulatory Commission (NRC) is focused on activities in support of nuclear power plant vulnerability assessments including aircraft vulnerability studies, emergency response and consequence assessments, cyber security studies associated with nuclear power pants, risk-informed vulnerability assessment, and testing reactor accidents. The NRC is dedicated to protecting the public and the environment from terrorist use of radiation from nuclear reactors, materials, or waste facilities.

Thus far, the Army Corps of Engineers has identified vulnerabilities at more than 300 locks and dams and has begun security modifications at the highest priority dams. Similarly, the Department of Interior's Bureau of Reclamation increased its security measures at high-priority dams and has begun security modifications at its 55 most critical facilities. Dam failure from a terrorist attack could lead to significant property damage or loss of life.

The Department of Interior also protects the nation's significant landmarks and monuments. DOI is the lead federal department with primary jurisdiction over national icons and monuments, such as the Statue of Liberty, Mt. Rushmore, Independence Hall, and the National Mall. To meet the requirements of increased security levels, the National Park Service will increase guard surveillance and security rehabilitation of national icons and monuments.

Increases requested over the FY 2003 enacted level for FY 2004 include:

- +$70 million for DOE to safeguard nuclear materials and facilities, secure transportation of nuclear materials, and improve material control and accountability.

- +$28 million for Interior to improve security at national monuments and icons; and

- +$8 million for EPA grants to fund drinking/waste water vulnerability assessments.

Challenges

As the focal point for assessing critical infrastructure vulnerabilities and prioritizing protective measures, IAIP faces a complex task. It will have to integrate intelligence with infrastructure information, better understand infrastructure interdependencies, and focus efforts on the highest priority protective measures.

IAIP will implement a clear plan for working with other agencies, state and local governments, and the private sector to build a comprehensive critical infrastructure and key asset assessment to facilitate the prioritization of risk mitigation measures. At the same time, DHS will have to balance the many sensitivities related to developing and maintaining such an assessment.

IAIP will also work with other federal and regulatory entities to clarify responsibilities to maintain full infrastructure coverage. IAIP and other federal agencies must clarify the relationships among themselves, and between the federal government and the state, local, and private sectors, to delineate responsibilities for protecting critical infrastructure and key assets.

HOMELAND SECURITY:
DEFENDING AGAINST CATASTROPHIC THREATS

Funding Summary – Defending Against Catastrophic Threats

Defending Against Catastrophic Threats
(budget authority in millions of dollars)

	2002 Enacted	2002 Supplemental	2003 Enacted	2003 Supplemental	2004 Request
Department of Commerce	56.7	0.8	63.9	---	72.3
Department of Defense	133.0	---	105.0	---	78.0
Department of Health and Human Services	95.3	97.1	1,643.7	---	1,741.5
Department of Homeland Security	70.0	77.0	488.0	6.5	674.0
Department of Justice	3.2	12.9	18.0	---	18.1
Department of State	---	11.0	---	---	---
Department of Transportation	0.7	4.0	---	---	---
National Science Foundation	9.0	---	27.0	---	27.0
Nuclear Regulatory Commission	---	---	---	---	12.1
Total, Defending Against Catastrophic Threats...	**367.8**	**202.8**	**2,345.6**	**6.5**	**2,623.0**

Major Agency Roles and Missions Summary – Defending Against Catastrophic Threats

Department/ Agency	Major Agency Roles and Missions
Commerce	*Bureau of Industry and Security* • Improve national and international export control of weapons, materials that may be used to construct weapons, and other technologies *National Institute of Standards and Technology* • Develop standards for devices that address CBRN threats
Defense	• Perform research and development related to chemical and biological threats
Health & Human Services	*National Institutes of Health* • Conduct basic and applied research related to likely bioterrorism agents • Design and test diagnostics, therapies, and vaccines • Maintain laboratory capacity and provide expert assistance to address bioterrorism and other WMD threats
Homeland Security	*Science and Technology* • Develop and test technologies and systems to detect CBRN materials and high explosives • Develop and test forensic methods to analyze CBRN materials and high explosives • Prioritize measures to address catastrophic threats through research and modeling • Develop standards for devices that address CBRN threats • Rapidly prototype homeland security technologies
Nuclear Regulatory Commission	• Improve security and control of nuclear fuels

Strategic Context – Defending Against Catastrophic Threats

The expertise, technology, and material needed to build chemical, biological, radiological, and nuclear (CBRN), weapons are proliferating. An attack involving a CBRN weapon or involving a

CBRN source could cause large numbers of casualties, mass psychological disruption, widespread contamination, and could overwhelm local medical capabilities. CBRN detection capabilities are dispersed throughout the country at every level of government. This category captures efforts to detect CBRN threats, treat casualties caused by them, and control the proliferation of CBRN sources. This category dovetails into border and transportation security, domestic counterterrorism, protecting critical infrastructure and key assets, and emergency preparedness and response as detection technologies are fielded and integrated into broader processes.

Defending Against Catastrophic Threats Activities

The President's Budget for defending against catastrophic threats activities increases from $373 million enacted in FY 2002 to $2.7 billion proposed for FY 2004. The largest increases are in the Department of Health and Human Services (+$1.6 billion) for defense against bioterrorism, including the development of vaccines, antimicrobials, and antidotes, and the Department of Homeland Security (+$604 million) to improve CBRN detection sensors and systems. For FY 2004, the budget requests a $290 million (12 percent) increase over FY 2003.

For FY 2004, HHS would fund roughly 65 percent of the activities designed to defend against catastrophic threats. Most of this funding falls within the National Institutes of Health (NIH), which continues to conduct basic and applied research related to likely bioterrorism agents. Funding is used for innovative research on genomics, and the design and testing of next generation diagnostics, therapies, vaccines, and infrastructure improvements.

Though funding for basic research and development (R&D) efforts may yield results over a longer time frame, HHS recently announced a breakthrough in developing a vaccine to protect against Ebola. HHS' requested increase in R&D funding[6] for FY 2004 over FY 2003 ($817 million, or 98 percent) overlaps with funding reported for defending against catastrophic threats, and reflects a shift from developing the "bricks and mortar" infrastructure to perform R&D (not categorized as R&D) to increased support for research efforts.

DHS funding for defending against catastrophic threats resides mainly in the Science and Technology Directorate (S&T). Whereas HHS focuses on basic research, DHS' current activities are focused on delivering operational capabilities to end-users in DHS, other federal agencies, state and local governments, and the private sector. S&T's Chemical, Biological, Radiological and Nuclear, and High Explosives countermeasures portfolios aim to develop technologies and broader systems to detect these threats, both to improve early warning capabilities and to facilitate investigation and attribution of materials (e.g., where was a specific agent produced). S&T's Rapid Prototyping, State and Local Standards, and Support to DHS Components portfolios are designed to speed the development of technology for use in the field, provide confidence in the effectiveness of technologies, and facilitate forward-thinking research within DHS.

Over the past year, in partnership with other federal agencies including HHS and EPA, S&T established the Biowatch program. In many metropolitan areas across the country, Biowatch

---

[6] See page 17

employs devices to detect terrorist agents like anthrax in time to provide early warning of a terrorist attack. S&T also developed guidelines for technical performance and testing of radiation detection equipment.

Funding increases for the S&T Directorate in DHS requested for FY 2004 over FY 2003 include:

- +$36 million for chemical countermeasures.

- +$62 million for radiological and nuclear countermeasures.

- +$35 million for support to DHS components' R&D efforts.

- +$20 million for state and local standards.

Other departments play a role in defending against catastrophic threats. Commerce's Bureau of Industry and Security requests a $3 million increase over FY 2003 in the mission area to combat proliferation of dangerous materials and its National Institute of Standards and Technology is seeking a $5 million increase for radiological and nuclear detection capabilities. The Nuclear Regulatory Commission requests a $12 million increase enhance controls of radiological resources.

Challenges

Agency efforts focus on developing systems to detect and respond to catastrophic threats. To best allocate resources, agencies must work together, avoid duplication of effort, and prioritize the capacities we are seeking to build government-wide based on the risks posed by specific catastrophic threats and the requirements for countering them. The Office of Science and Technology Policy, Homeland Security Council, and the Technical Support Working Group coordinate crosscutting efforts to ensure this is the case. The Biowatch program is an example of a multi-agency crosscutting effort; such collaboration improves our nation's ability to defend against catastrophic threats.

In addition, this collaboration must extend to operational agencies to develop broader end-to-end systems for countering catastrophic threats. The Department of Homeland Security's Science and Technology Directorate's role as an end-user-oriented organization will help to facilitate technology development, but technology development should not be viewed in isolation. It must be prioritized as part of an integrated system to improve border and transportation security, domestic counterterrorism, protecting critical infrastructure and key assets, and emergency preparedness and response. To that end, DHS's Science and Technology Directorate, in partnership with other federal agencies, has a significant challenge in developing for technologies that may be used by the federal government, state and local governments, or the private sector.

HOMELAND SECURITY:
EMERGENCY PREPAREDNESS AND RESPONSE

Funding Summary – Emergency Preparedness and Response

Emergency Preparedness and Response
(budget authority in millions of dollars)

	2002 Enacted	2002 Supplemental	2003 Enacted	2003 Supplemental	2004 Request
Department of Agriculture	5.6	41.4	11.7	---	15.3
Department of Commerce	16.5	1.0	15.1	---	29.6
Department of Defense--Military	217.0	25.0	213.0	---	172.0
Department of Energy	98.9	17.4	120.9	---	89.7
Department of Health and Human Services	191.0	1,323.1	1,777.6	142.0	1,851.7
Department of Homeland Security	328.7	1,770.7	1,486.7	2,130.0	4,875.3
Department of the Interior	3.5	---	4.2	---	4.2
Department of Justice	0.2	259.0	10.5	---	2.3
Department of Labor	5.4	---	5.2	---	4.2
Department of State	---	1.0	8.0	---	1.0
Department of Transportation	5.3	13.4	12.5	---	15.2
Department of the Treasury	21.4	15.0	15.1	---	15.8
Department of Veterans Affairs	19.2	---	57.2	---	16.9
Corps of Engineers-Civil Works	---	39.0	---	---	---
Environmental Protection Agency	3.2	39.3	13.1	---	28.0
General Services Administration	0.9	---	1.8	---	2.0
Office of Personnel Management	0.8	---	---	---	0.5
Corporation for National and Community Service	29.0	---	57.0	---	118.0
District of Columbia	13.0	174.0	25.0	---	15.0
Postal Service	---	180.5	---	---	---
Total, Emergency Preparedness and Response	**959.5**	**3,899.8**	**3,834.6**	**2,272.0**	**7,256.6**

Major Agency Roles and Missions Summary – Emergency Preparedness and Response

Department/ Agency	Major Agency Roles and Missions
Agriculture	• Prepare for and respond to agricultural emergencies in cooperation with state and local governments • Maintain agency response capability for agricultural emergencies
Commerce	• Develop standards for first responder activities
Defense	• Maintain WMD response teams to support civil authorities
Energy	• Maintain radiological and nuclear response capabilities
Homeland Security	• Support terrorism preparedness training and equipment for state and local first responders • Support state and local planning and mutual aid activities • Assess, exercise, and evaluate state and local preparedness levels • Support improvements to state and local emergency operations facilities and communications systems • Promote communications interoperability • Lead the development and implementation of the National Response Plan and the National Incident Management System • Maintain the Strategic National Stockpile, National Disaster Medical System, and Urban Search and Rescue teams • Build the Citizens Corps

Health and Human Services	• Support state and local public health planning activities • Support training and equipment to improve state and local public health capability • Assess, exercise, and evaluate state and local public heath preparedness levels • Support to improvements to state and local communications and health information systems • Prepare heathcare providers for catastrophic terrorism • Maintain department response capability for public health emergencies in cooperation with state and local governments
Transportation	• Maintain crisis-management capability
Veterans Affairs	• Support public health preparedness activities
EPA	• Maintain teams to respond to a CBRN event • Maintain capability to perform CBRN decontamination
CNCS	• Encourage volunteer and citizen participation in emergency preparedness and response activities

Strategic Context – Emergency Preparedness and Response

The Emergency Preparedness and Response category captures agency efforts to prepare for and respond to major incidents and disasters, particularly terrorist attacks that would endanger lives and property or disrupt federal operations. The mission area encompasses the broad range of agency incident management activities, as well assistance to states and localities for similar purposes, and related R&D activities to develop systems and technologies for operational end users. These efforts are also being integrated as part of a consolidated National Response Plan and National Incident Management System.

As outlined in the *National Strategy for Homeland Security*, the goal is to plan, equip, train, and exercise response units to mobilize to respond to both natural and man-made disasters. State and local governments have key roles in fulfilling this mission, most essentially through their support of first responders, emergency management, and public health infrastructure. The federal government is leveraging this array of resources and capabilities through both financial assistance and the coordination of activities at each level of government.

Agency Roles, Funding, and Accomplishments

Funding for federal emergency preparedness and response activities have increased dramatically over the past two years, reaching a total of $7.3 billion in the President's FY 2004 Budget. This level is more than seven times the amount provided in FY 2002 and 89 percent the FY 2003 enacted level. Although DHS and HHS are requesting 93 percent of the resources in this mission area, 16 other agencies also participate. As indicated in the major roles and missions summary, many maintain more specialized response capabilities that could be employed to respond to specific threats.

Emergency preparedness and response funding has grown significantly in the Departments of Homeland Security (+$4.5 billion, or more than 1,000 percent, from FY 2002 to FY 2004) and Health and Human Services (+$1.7 billion, or almost 900 percent, from FY 2002 to FY 2004). Much of this funding growth is attributable to federal assistance to state and local preparedness and response. These agencies have initiated major state and local grant programs to equip and train first responders and prepare the public heath infrastructure for a range of potential threats, especially terrorism.

This increase in emergency preparedness funding has supported:

- Allocation of nearly $8 billion in state and local grant funding from the Departments of Homeland Security, Health and Human Services, and Justice in FYs 2002 and 2003.

- Training for nearly 300,000 first responders through the Departments of Justice and Homeland Security.

- Over 165 terrorism preparedness exercises, including the largest preparedness exercise in American history -- TOPOFF II.

- Work on the National Response Plan, which supports the development of a comprehensive National Incident Management System.

- Stockpiling vaccines and pharmaceuticals so that all Americans can be vaccinated for smallpox, and 20 million persons exposed to anthrax can be treated.

- Developing terrorism preparedness plans and public health preparedness plans for every state.

Major DHS initiatives in FY 2004 include:

- Continuing implementation of the $3.6 billion (in FY 2004) First Responder Initiative to provide coordinated terrorism preparedness training and equipment for state and local responders across the various responder agencies.

- +$890 million (and a total of $5.6 billion over ten years) for Project BioShield to spur the development and purchase of vaccines and other critical countermeasures; and $400 million for maintaining and strengthening the Strategic National Stockpile. These programs will ensure that critical pharmaceutical countermeasures are readily available and rapidly distributed in case of a biological or radiological attack.

HHS has the lead role in preparing public health providers for catastrophic terrorism, including the $518 million provided to states for hospital infrastructure and mutual aid through the Health Resources and Services Administration, (HRSA), and $940 million provided to states through the Centers for Disease Control and Prevention (CDC) for upgrades to state and local public health capacity.

Challenges

Concurrent with these major state and local investments, DHS, HHS and other agencies maintain their own preparedness and response functions. These include incident management, continuity of operations, and emergency notification activities. A key element of the national strategy is to merge these disparate efforts, and their underlying response plans, into a single all-hazards incident management plan coordinated by the Department of Homeland Security.

The most significant challenge facing emergency preparedness and response is measuring actual improvements in the nation's readiness level. Given the wide range of threats and contingencies, we will decide what gaps should be addressed first and how will we know when we are prepared. Such measures are needed to balance the relative threats of attacks and disasters with available resource requirements. The Department of Homeland Security, in cooperation with other agencies, will establish readiness measures and standards that contribute to a more thorough assessment of federal, state, and local capabilities. These standards will be incorporated into terrorism and emergency preparedness exercises, and grant programs.

Such standards and measures are critical given the unprecedented levels of federal support for state and local planning, training, exercises, and equipment acquisition. These investments are not intended to support normal operating expenses but rather to build the capacity and capability to respond to major events. The initial means of ensuring that federal funds are targeted properly is to ensure that assistance is allocated based on state preparedness plans and focused on those areas facing the greatest risks, vulnerabilities, and potential consequences. Over the coming months, DHS will work with other federal agencies to apply the standards and measures under development to state and local efforts.

The Administration has sought to avoid duplicative and overlapping programs by taking a number of steps, including planning, interagency agreements, and program consolidation. For example, DHS is integrating the planning procedures overseen by the Office for Domestic Preparedness, Emergency Preparedness and Response, and TSA. DHS and HHS have signed agreements to coordinate their respective reviews of state funding applications and management of the Strategic National Stockpile. While some progress has been made over the last two years to better integrate overlapping grant programs, more remains to be done. The President's FY 2004 Budget proposes to consolidate grants for emergency managers and fire departments.

OTHER HOMELAND SECURITY

Homeland Security Funding for Other Activities
(budget authority in millions of dollars)

	2002 Enacted	2002 Supplemental	2003 Enacted	2003 Supplemental	2004 Request
Department of Energy....................................	15.0	---	---	---	---
Department of Homeland Security.................	89.7	13.3	122.6	---	197.4
Environmental Protection Agency...................	0.6	---	49.7	---	8.3
Executive Office of the President activities.....	2.0	138.0	41.0	---	35.0
Total, Other Activities.........................	**107.3**	**151.3**	**213.3**	**---**	**240.7**

Strategic Context – Other Homeland Security

The Other Homeland Security category captures those activities that do not fit neatly into the original six mission areas defined in the *National Strategy for Homeland Security*. As such, activities in this category are not part of an overarching theme or mission, but are a mix of programs not easily categorized elsewhere. In some cases, these activities will likely be aggregated with others in the future and/or disaggregated in order to facilitate categorization.

Agency Roles, Funding, and Accomplishments

Eighty-two percent of other homeland security funding is reported by DHS. Within DHS, major activities with relatively constant funding reported in the Other Homeland Security category include security and infrastructure improvements to the DHS headquarters facilities, and Congressionally-mandated programs administered through the Office for Domestic Preparedness. Increases in DHS' Other Homeland Security activities occurred primarily in homeland security-related technology investments, partnership programs designed to promote homeland security research and development, and other partnership programs focused on better understanding of international, national, and state infrastructure.

Most of the remaining Other Homeland Security funding is within Executive Office of the President (EOP) and the Environmental Protection Agency. EOP funding supports the Homeland Security Council and ensures the security of the White House complex and other EOP entities.

Challenges

As OMB continues to work with federal agencies to collect data related to combating terrorism missions, it should focus on categorizing all programs within the critical mission areas identified in the *National Strategy for Homeland Security*. While the Other Homeland Security category accounts for only six-tenths of one percent of the government's homeland security spending, OMB plans to work with respondent agencies to reduce funds reported in this category.

www.ingramcontent.com/pod-product-compliance
Lightning Source LLC
Chambersburg PA
CBHW080624290526
45790CB00007B/2914